MW00906914

Keto Bread Cookbook – The Complete Guide

200 Ketogenic Low-Carb Recipes To Make Easily At Your Home. From Basic To Sweet, All Recipes Are Delicious And Perfect For Any Meal And Occasion

Sarah Miller

© **Copyright 2021 – Sarah Miller - All rights reserved**

This document is geared towards providing exact and reliable information in regards to the topic and issue covered. The publication is sold with the idea that the publisher is not required to render accounting, officially permitted, or otherwise qualified services. If advice is necessary, legal or professional, a practiced individual in the profession should be ordered.

From a Declaration of Principles which was accepted and approved equally by a Committee of the American Bar Association and a Committee of Publishers and Associations.

In no way is it legal to reproduce, duplicate, or transmit any part of this document in either electronic means or printed format. Recording of this publication is strictly prohibited, and any storage of this document is not allowed unless with written permission from the publisher. All rights reserved.

The information provided herein is stated to be truthful and consistent, any liability, in terms of inattention or otherwise, by any usage or abuse of any policies, processes, or directions contained within is the solitary and utter responsibility of the recipient reader. Under no circumstances will any legal responsibility or blame be held against the publisher for any reparation, damages, or monetary loss due to the information herein, either directly or indirectly.

Respective authors own all copyrights not held by the publisher.

The information herein is offered for informational purposes solely and is universal as so.

The presentation of the information is without contract or any type of guarantee assurance.

The trademarks that are used are without any consent, and the publication of the trademark is without permission or backing by the trademark owner. All trademarks and brands within this book are for clarifying purposes only and belong to the owners themselves, not affiliated with this document.

TABLE OF CONTENTS

INTRODUCTION

Keto bread is a low-carbohydrate, high-fat liquid diet plan that requires you to consume a lot of healthy fats through either a keto bread recipe book or diet program. It's short for the controversial low-carbohydrate ketogenic diet more commonly referred to as the ketogenic diet. There are many variations of the keto diet with different levels of restrictions. For example, some people may only get 20 grams of carbohydrates per day while others restrict their intake to 5 grams of carbohydrates per day. The keto diet can be used as a short term diet, but most people choose to follow it for more than a month.

How Does Keto Bread Help You Lose Weight?

The idea behind the keto bread diet is that when you eat lots of healthy fats such as butter, olive oil, avocados, macadamia nuts, eggs, and grass-fed meats you will lose weight quickly and easily. The key to losing weight fast with this kind of eating plan is to take in so many calories through fat that you end up burning off the extra calories you burned from food intake. The keto bread diet plan isn't hard to follow if you stick to the rules. It's just a matter of cutting out most carbs and eating lots of healthy fats.

Is Eating Keto Bread Right For You?

If you want to lose weight fast and lose it completely with no chance of gaining it back then the keto bread recipe book or ketogenic diet might be right for you. It's not right for everyone though and can't be used in place of other methods like exercise and eating less food on your own as part of your weight loss program. If you're going to use this kind of eating plan make sure you check w/ your doctor first to see if it's right for you before putting it into action

The Keto diet has become more popular in the last few years. It is a low-carb, high-fat eating style that has been highly researched and proven to be effective. Here at Keto Bread, we have all of the necessary tools for anyone who is interested in changing their eating patterns to something healthier, such as the Men's Standard Keto Cookbook. We understand that everyone's nutritional needs are different, so we have cataloged a wide variety of recipes to meet your needs. Keto is a deficient carbohydrate diet with ample protein, which is allowed during the diet. It is not just a ketogenic change in the diet and grows healthy eating habits. They create healthy and natural eating habits for you stronger both physically and mentally. Our body needs energy as it is coming from carbohydrates; our body uses glucose (carbohydrates) as a primary energy source.

The ketogenic diet is a low-calorie, high-fat diet in which fat is converted into energy instead of glucose. During this process, fatty acids are released from your body, and our liver renovates these fatty acids into ketones. When ketone levels have increased in the blood goes to the brain and replaces glucose with energy. You can reach this stage in the first week of the ketogenic diet.

The keto diet is not new, but its popularity has declined over time as various medical developments seem to help with conditions like epilepsy and weight loss. However, now, people are again beginning to see it as a way to lose weight, lighten skin, maintain their health, and even live longer. So much to wait for!

Our body uses glucose as its primary source of energy. Never Carbohydrates are metabolized, and glucose is produced in our body. This glucose is stored in the cells of our body. When glucose levels rise, then the excess glucose is converted to glycogen. This chemical process of the conversion of glucose to glycogen is called glycogenesis. This glycogen is stored in the muscles of the body and liver as a backup source of energy. In this diet, your body undergoes many adjustments. Some different signs and symptoms confirm that you are in ketosis.

BASIC BREAD

1. MILK ALMOND BREAD

Preparation time: 3 ½ hours - Cooking time: 3 ½ hours - Servings: 8

Ingredients: 1 ¼ cup milk - 5 ¼ cups almond flour - 2 tablespoons butter - 2 teaspoons dry yeast - 1 tablespoon sugar - 2 teaspoons salt

Directions: Pour the milk into the form and ½ cup of water. Add flour. Put butter, sugar, and salt in different corners of the mold. Make a groove in the flour and put in the yeast. Bake on the Basic program. Cool the bread.

Nutrition: Carbohydrates: 5 g / Fats: 4.5 g / Protein: 10.1 g / Calories: 352 / Fiber: 1, 5 g

2. KETO BREAD

Preparation time: 15 minutes - Cooking time: 40 minServings: 6

Ingredients: 2 cups fine ground almond dinner (from whitened almonds) - 2 teaspoons preparing powder - 1/2 teaspoon fine Himalayan salt - 1/2 cup olive oil or avocado oil 1/2 cup separated water - 5 large eggs - 1 tablespoon poppy seeds

Directions: You will require a hand blender, portion dish, and material paper. Pre-heat stove to 400°F. Line portion container with material paper. In a large bowl, combine the almond dinner, preparing powder and salt. While as yet blending, shower in the avocado oil until a brittle batter structure. Make a well (little gap) in the mixture. Air out the eggs into the well, add the water and beat together, making little circles with your blender in the eggs until light yellow and foamy. Then, start making greater circles to fuse the almond feast and blend into it. Continue blending like this, until it would appear that flapjack hitter— Smooth, light, and thick. Empty the blend into the portion container, use a spatula to scratch it full scale. Sprinkle the poppy seeds on top. Heat for 40 minutes in the middle rack. It will be hard, raised, and brilliant dark colored when done. Remove from the broiler and let it sit for 30 minutes to cool. Then, unmold and cut it. Store in water/air proof compartment in the ice chest as long as 5 days. Toast to warm!

Nutrition: Calories: 270 / Fat: 15 g / Fiber: 3 g / Carbs: 5 g / Protein: 9 g

3. SAUSAGE BREAD

Preparation time: 4 hours - Cooking time: 4 hours - Servings: 8

Ingredients: 1 ½ teaspoon dry yeast - 3 cups flour - 1 teaspoon sugar - 1 ½ teaspoons salt 1 1/3 cups whey - 1 tablespoon oil - 1 cup chopped smoked sausage

Directions: Add all the ingredients in the order that is recommended specifically for your model. Set the required parameters for Baking bread. When ready, remove the delicious hot bread. Wait for it to cool down and enjoy with sausage.

Nutrition: Carbohydrates: 4 g / Fats: 5.1 g / Protein: 7.4 g / Calories: 234 / Fiber: 1.3 g

4. GLUTEN-FREE CHOCOLATE ZUCCHINI BREAD

Preparation time: 5 minutes - Cooking time: 10 minutes - Servings: 12

Ingredients: 1 ½ cups coconut flour - ¼ cup unsweetened cocoa powder - ½ cup erythritol ½ teaspoon cinnamon - 1 teaspoon baking soda - 1 teaspoon baking powder - ¼ teaspoon salt ¼ cup coconut oil, melted - 4 eggs - 1 teaspoon vanilla - 2 cups zucchini, shredded

Directions: Shred the zucchini and use paper towels to drain excess water, set aside. Lightly beat eggs with coconut oil, then add to bread machine pan. Add the remaining ingredients to the pan. Set bread machine to Gluten-free. When the bread is done, remove the bread machine pan from the bread machine. Let it cool slightly before transferring to a cooling rack. You can store your bread for up to 5 days.

Nutrition: Calories: 185 / Carbohydrates: 6 g / Fats: 17 g / Protein: 5 g

5. ZUCCHINI BREAD

Preparation time: 2 hours 10 min. - Cooking time: 2 hours 10 minutes - Servings: 8

Ingredients: 2 whole eggs - ¼ teaspoon sea salt - 1 cup olive oil - 1 cup white sugar 1 tablespoon vanilla sugar - 2 teaspoons cinnamon - ½ cup nuts, ground - 3 cups bread flour, well sifted - 1 tablespoon baking powder - 1¼ cup zucchini, grated

Directions: Prepare all of the ingredients for your bread and measuring utensils (a cup, a spoon, kitchen scales). Carefully measure the ingredients into the pan, except the zucchini and nuts. Place all the ingredients into the bread bucket in the right order, following the manual for your bread machine. Close the cover. Select the program of your bread machine to Cake and choose the crust color to Light. Press Start. After the signal, put the grated zucchini and nuts into the dough. Wait until the program completes. When done, take the bucket out and let it cool for 5-10 minutes. Shake the loaf from the pan and let it cool for 30 minutes on a cooling rack. Slice, serve, and enjoy the taste of fragrant homemade bread.

Nutrition: Carbohydrates: 4 g / Fats: 31 g / Protein: 8.6 g / Calories: 556 / Fiber: 1.3 g

6. EGG COCONUT BREAD

Preparation time: 10 minutes - Cooking time: 40 minutes - Servings: 4

Ingredients: ½ cup coconut flour - 4 eggs - 1 cup water - 2 tablespoons apple cider vinegar ¼ teaspoon salt - ¼ cup coconut oil, plus 1 teaspoon melted - ½ teaspoon garlic powder ½ teaspoon baking soda

Directions: Preheat the oven to 350°F. Grease a baking tin with 1 teaspoon coconut oil. Set aside. Add eggs to a blender along with vinegar, water, and ¼-cup coconut oil. Blend for 30 sec. Add coconut flour, baking soda, garlic powder, and salt. Blend for 1 minute. Transfer to the baking tin. Bake for 40 minutes. Enjoy.

Nutrition: Calories: 297 / Fat: 14 g / Carb: 9 g / Protein: 15 g

7. APPLE BUTTER BREAD

Preparation time: 2 hours - Cooking time: 25 minutes - Servings: 10

Ingredients: ½ cup unsalt melted butter - 1 cup swerve sweetener - 1 egg - 1 cup unsweetened apple butter - 1 teaspoon of cinnamon powder - 2 cups almond flour - 2 teaspoons baking soda 1 teaspoon nutmeg ground - 1 teaspoon extract of vanilla - ½ cup of unsweetened almond milk 2 teaspoons of active dry yeast

Directions: Mix the almond flour, Swerve, cinnamon, nutmeg powder, and baking soda in a container. Get another container and combine the unsweetened apple butter, unsalted melted butter, vanilla essence, and almond milk that are unsweetened. As per the instructions on the manual of your machine, pour the ingredients in the bread pan, taking care to follow how to mix in the yeast. Place the bread pan in the machine and select the Sweet bread setting, together with the crust type, if available, then press Start once you have closed the lid of the machine. When the bread is ready, using oven mitts, remove the bread pan from the machine. Use a stainless spatula to extract the bread from the pan and turn the pan upside down on a metallic rack where the bread will cool off before slicing it.

Nutrition: Calories: 217 / Fat: 13 g / Carb: 42 g / Protein: 4 g

8. COCONUT MILK BREAD

Preparation time: 3 hours - Cooking time: 3 hours - Servings: 10

Ingredients: 1 whole egg - ½ cup lukewarm milk - ½ cup lukewarm coconut milk ¼ cup butter, melted and cooled - 2 tablespoons liquid honey - 4 cups almond flour, sifted 1 tablespoon active dry yeast - 1 teaspoon salt - ½ cup coconut chips

Directions: Prepare all the ingredients for your bread and measuring utensils (a cup, a spoon, kitchen scales). Carefully measure the ingredients into the pan, except the coconut chips. Place all the ingredients into the bread bucket in the right order, following the manual for your bread machine. Close the cover. Select the program of the bread machine to Sweet and choose the crust color to Medium. Press Start. After the signal, add the coconut chips into the dough. Wait until the program completes. When done, take the bucket out and let it cool for 5-10 minutes. Shake the loaf from the pan and let it cool for 30 minutes on a cooling rack. Slice, serve, and enjoy the taste of fragrant homemade bread.

Nutrition: Carbohydrates: 6 g / Fats: 15.3 g / Protein: 9.5 g / Calories: 421 / Fiber: 1.6 g

9. CHEESE SAUSAGE BREAD

Preparation time: 4 hours - Cooking time: 4 hours - Servings: 8

Ingredients: 1 teaspoon dry yeast - 3 ½ cups flour - 1 teaspoon salt - 1 tablespoon sugar
1 cup water - 1 ½ tablespoon oil - 2 tablespoons smoked sausage - 2 tablespoons grated cheese
1 tablespoon chopped garlic

Directions: Cut the sausage into small cubes. Grate the cheese on a grater; chop the garlic. Add the ingredients to the bread machine according to the instructions. Turn on the baking program, and let it do the work.

Nutrition: Carbohydrates: 4 g / Fats: 5.6 g / Protein: 7.7 g / Calories: 260 / Fiber: 1.3 g

10. LEMON BLUEBERRY BREAD

Preparation time: 2 hours - Cooking time: 25 minutes - Servings: 10

Ingredients: 2 cups almond flour - 1/2 cup coconut flour - 1/2 cup ghee - 1/2 cup coconut oil, melted - 1/2 cup erythritol - 4 eggs - 2 tablespoons lemon zest, about half a lemon - 1 teaspoon lemon juice - 1/2 cup blueberries - 2 teaspoons baking powder

Directions: Lightly beat eggs before pouring them into your bread machine pan. Add in melted coconut oil, ghee, and lemon juice to the pan. Add the remaining dry ingredients including blueberries and lemon zest to the bread machine pan. Set bread machine to Quick bread setting. When the bread is done, remove the bread machine pan from the bread machine. Let it cool slightly before transferring to a cooling rack. You can store your bread for up to 5 days.

Nutrition: Calories: 300 / Carbohydrates: 14 g / Protein: 5 g / Fat: 30 g

11. SWEET COFFEE BREAD

Preparation time: 2 hours - Cooking time: 25 minutes - Servings: 10

Ingredients: 2 cups of almond fine flour - ½ teaspoon salt - Cinnamon, three-quarters of a teaspoon - 4 eggs - ½ cup Swerve Keto sweetener - ½ cup of unsalted melted butter
¼ cup of protein powder that is not flavored - 4 teaspoons of coconut flour - 2/3 cup of almond milk that is not sweetened - 2 teaspoons espresso - ½ teaspoon extract from vanilla
2 teaspoons active dry yeast - 2 teasp. baking powder

Directions: Mix together the almond flour, coconut flour, sweetener Swerve, cinnamon, salt, baking powder, espresso, and unflavored protein powder in a container. Mix the unsweetened almond milk, eggs, extract of vanilla, and unsalted melted butter in another container. As per the instructions on the manual of your machine, pour the ingredients in the bread pan, taking care to follow how to mix in the yeast. Place the bread pan in the machine, and select the Sweet bread setting, together with the crust type, if available, then press Start once you have closed the lid of the machine. When the bread is ready, extract it from the pan and place it on a wire mesh surface to cool before cutting it.

Nutrition: Calories: 177.7 / Fat: 3.8 g / Carb: 31 g / Protein: 4.6 g

12. BREAD WITH BEEF

Preparation time: 2 hours - Cooking time: 2 hours - Servings: 6

Ingredients: 5 oz. beef - 15 oz. almond flour - 5 oz. rye flour - 1 onion - 3 teaspoons dry yeast 5 tablespoons olive oil - 1 tablespoon sugar - Sea salt - Ground black pepper

Directions: Pour the warm water into the 15 oz. of the wheat flour and rye flour and leave overnight. Chop the onions and cut the beef into cubes. Fry the onions until clear and golden brown and then mix in the bacon and fry on low heat for 20 minutes until soft. Combine the yeast with the warm water, mixing until smooth consistency, and then combine the yeast with the flour, salt and sugar, but don't forget to mix and knead well. Add in the fried onions with the beef and black pepper and mix well. Pour some oil into a bread machine and place the dough into the bread maker. Cover the dough with the towel and leave for 1 hour. Close the lid and turn the bread machine on the Basic/white bread program. Bake the bread until the medium crust and after the bread is ready take it out and leave for 1 hour covered with the towel and only then you can slice the bread.

Nutrition: Carbohydrates: 6 g / Fats: 21 g / Protein: 13 g / Calories: 299 / Fiber: 1.6 g

13. CINNAMON CAKE

Preparation time: 7 minutes - Cooking time: 5 minutes - Servings: 12

Ingredients: ½ cup erythritol - ½ cup butter - ½ tablespoon vanilla extract - 1 ¾ cups almond flour - 1 ½ teaspoon baking powder - 1 ½ teaspoon cinnamon - ¼ teaspoon sea salt 1 ½ cup carrots, grated - 1 cup pecans, chopped

Directions: Grate carrots and place them in a food processor. Add in the rest of the ingredients, except the pecans, and process until well incorporated. Fold in pecans. Pour mixture into bread machine pan. Set bread machine to bake. When baking is completed, remove from the bread machine and transfer to a cooling rack. Allow cooling completely before slicing. (You can also top with a sugar-free cream cheese frosting, see recipe below). You can store for up to 5 days in the refrigerator.

Nutrition: Calories: 350 / Carbohydrates: 8 g / Fats: 34 g / Protein: 7 g

14. GREAT FLAVOR CHEESE BREAD WITH THE ADDED KICK OF PIMENTO OLIVES

Preparation time: 5 minutes - Cooking time: 3 hours - Servings: 1 loaf

Ingredients: 1 cup water room temperature - 4 teaspoons sugar - 3/4 teaspoon salt 1 ¼ cups shredded sharp Cheddar cheese - 3 cups bread flour 2 teaspoons active dry yeast - 3/4 cup pimiento olives, drained and sliced

Directions: Add all ingredients except olives to the machine pan. Select Basic bread setting. At prompt before second knead, mix in olives.

Nutrition: Calories: 124 / Total fat: 4 g (2 g sat. fat) / Carb. 19 g / Fiber: 1 g / Protein: 5 g

15. WILD RICE CRANBERRY BREAD

Preparation time: 5 minutes - Cooking time: 3 hours - Servings: 1 loaf

Ingredients: 1 ¼ cup water - ¼ cup skim milk powder - 1 ¼ teaspoon salt - 2 tablespoons liquid honey - 1 tablespoon extra-virgin olive oil - 3 cups all-purpose flour - 3/4 cup cooked wild rice - 1/4 cup pine nuts - ¾ teaspoon celery seeds - 1/8 teaspoon freshly ground black pepper 1 teaspoon bread machine or instant yeast - 2/3 cup dried cranberries

Directions: Add all ingredients to the machine pan except the cranberries. Place pan into the oven chamber. Select Basic bread setting. At the signal to add ingredients, add the cranberries.

Nutrition: Calories: 225 / Total fat: 7.8 g (1.2 g sat. fat) / Carb: 33 g / Fiber: 1 g / Protein: 6.7 g

16. FANTASTIC BREAD

Preparation time: 5 minutes - Cooking time: 20 min - Servings: 6

Ingredients: 1 cup almond flour or almond supper - 4 tablespoons entire psyllium husk 2 teaspoons of preparing powder - 1/2 teaspoon of salt (discretionary) little bunch almond fragments (discretionary) little bunch squashed pecans - 6 large eggs - 1 cup full-fat yogurt

Directions: Add the dry ingredients to a big blending bowl and mix. The nuts are discretionary or can fill in for different kinds of nuts on the off chance that you like. Crack 6 large eggs into a different blending bowl, add one cup full-fat yogurt, and blend well in with a hand blender. Add the dry blend and blend completely with a hand blender. Set it aside for 10–15 minutes while you preheat your broiler to 350° F. Rinse the material paper under warm water and shake it off before crushing it into your preparing tin, then add your blend to the tin and press it into the sides. You can add nuts like almonds, sesame seeds, and pumpkin seeds to the highest point of the portion and pop it into the stove for 55 minutes. Haul the bread out when completed and let it cool on a rack.

Nutrition: Calories: 40 / Carbs: 4 g / Net Carbs: 2.5 g / Fiber: 5.5 g / Fat: 9 g - Protein: 6 g

17. CHEESE CAULIFLOWER BROCCOLI BREAD

Preparation time: 10 minutes - Cooking time: 3 hours - Servings: 1 loaf

Ingredients: 1/4 cup water - 4 tablespoons oil - 1 egg white - 1 teaspoon lemon juice 2/3 cup grated Cheddar cheese - 3 Tablespoons green onion - 1/2 cup broccoli, chopped 1/2 cup cauliflower, chopped - 1/2 teaspoon lemon-pepper seasoning - 2 cup bread flour 1 teaspoon regular or quick-rising yeast

Directions: Add all ingredients to the machine pan. Select Basic bread setting.

Nutrition: Calories: 156 / Total fat: 7.4 g (2.2 g sat. fat) / Carb: 17 g / Fiber: 0 g / Protein: 4.9 g

18. RICOTTA CHIVE BREAD

Preparation time: 5 minutes - Cooking time: 3 hours - Servings: 1 loaf

Ingredients: 1 cup lukewarm water - 1/3 cup whole or part-skim ricotta cheese - 1 ½ teaspoon salt - 1 tablespoon granulated sugar - 3 cups bread flour - 1/2 cup chopped chives
2 ½ teaspoon instant yeast

Directions: Add ingredients to bread machine pan except for dried fruit. Choose the Basic bread setting and Light/medium crust.

Nutrition: Calories: 92 / Total fat: 0 (0 g sat. fat) / Carbs: 17 g / Fiber: 1 g / Protein: 3 g

19. KETO ENGLISH MUFFIN LOAF

Preparation time: 10 minutes - Cooking time: 3 hours - Total Time: 3 hours 10 min

Servings: 1-pound loaf of 8 slices

Ingredients: 1 cup warm water (80 °F) - 2 tablespoons Sugar - 3 tablespoons Non-fat dry milk
1 teaspoon salt - ¼ teaspoon baking soda - 2 ½ cups almond flour - 1 tablespoon vital wheat gluten - 1 ¾ teaspoon dry active yeast

Directions: Measure all the ingredients in the bread machine pan in the order listed above. Turn on the bread machine and process. Select Basic cycle; choose normal Crust Color setting. Close the lid and press the Start button. Once cooked, place bread in cooling rack. Slice, then toast and serve.

Nutrition: Calories: 22 / Calories from fat: 9 / Total Fat: 1 g / Total Carbohydrates: 3 g
Net Carbohydrates: 3 g / Protein: 2g

20. CELERY BREAD

Preparation time: 10 minutes - Cooking time: 3 hours - Servings: 1 loaf

Ingredients: 1 (10 oz.) can cream of celery soup - 3 tablespoons low-fat milk, heated
1 tablespoon vegetable oil - 1 ¼ teaspoon celery, garlic, or onion salt - 3/4 cup celery, fresh/slice thin - 1 tablespoon celery leaves, fresh, chopped -optional - 1 egg - 3 cups bread flour
1/4 teaspoon sugar - 1/4 teaspoon ginger - 1/2 cup quick-cooking oats - 2 tablespoons gluten
2 teaspoons celery seeds - 1 package active dry yeast

Directions: Add all ingredients to the machine pan. Select basic bread setting.

Nutrition: Calories: 73 / Total fat: 3.6 g (0 g sat. fat) / Carb: 8 g / Fiber: 0 / Protein: 2.6 g

21. ORANGE CAPPUCCINO BREAD

Preparation time: 10 minutes - Cooking time: 3 hours - Servings: 1 loaf

Ingredients: 1 cup water - 1 tablespoon instant coffee granules - 2 tablespoons butter or margarine, softened - 1 teaspoon grated orange peel - 3 cups Bread flour - 2 tablespoons dry milk - 1/4 cup sugar - 1 ¼ teaspoon salt - 2 ¼ teaspoon bread machine or quick active dry yeast

Directions: Add all ingredients to the machine pan. Select Basic bread setting.

Nutrition: Calories: 155 / Total fat: 2 g (1 g sat. fat) / Carb: 31 g / Fiber: 1 g / Protein: 4 g

22. RED HOT CINNAMON BREAD

Preparation time: 5 minutes - Cooking time: 3 hours - Servings: 1 loaf

Ingredients: 1/4 cup lukewarm water - 1/2 cup lukewarm milk - 1/4 cup softened butter
2 ¼ teaspoons instant yeast - 1 ¼ teaspoons salt - 1/4 cup sugar - 1 teaspoon vanilla
1 large egg, lightly beaten - 3 cups all-purpose flour - 1/2 cup Cinnamon Red Hot candies

Directions: Add ingredients to bread machine pan except for candy. Choose Dough setting. After the cycle is over, turn the dough out into bowl and cover, let it rise for 45 minutes to one hour. Gently punch down dough and shape into a rectangle. Knead in the cinnamon candies in 1/3 at a time. Shape the dough into a loaf and place in a greased or parchment-lined loaf pan. Line the pan loosely with lightly greased plastic wrap, and allow a second rise for 40-50 minutes. Preheat oven to 350°F. Bake 30-40 minutes. Remove and cool on a wire rack before slicing.

Nutrition: Calories: 207 / Total fat: 6.9 g / 4.1 g sat Fat / Carb: 30 g / Fiber: 1 g / Protein: 4.6 g

23. COTTAGE CHEESE BREAD

Preparation time: 10 minutes - Cooking time: 3 hours - Servings: 1 loaf

Ingredients: 1/2 cup water - 1 cup cottage cheese - 2 tablespoons margarine - 1 egg
1 tablespoon white sugar - 1/4 teaspoon baking soda - 1 teaspoon salt - 3 cups bread flour
2 ½ teaspoons active dry yeast

Directions: Add all ingredients to the machine pan. Follow the order suggested by the manufacturer. Select Basic bread setting. Tip: If the dough is too sticky, add up to ½ cup more flour.

Nutrition: Calories: 171 / Total fat: 3.6 g (1 g sat. fat) / Carb: 26 g / Fiber: 1 g / Protein: 7.3 g

24. EASY KETO BREAD

Preparation time: 9 minutes - Cooking time: 21 min - Servings: 5

Ingredients: 6 large eggs - 2/3 cup almond flour or almond supper - 1/3 cup coconut flour 3 teaspoon coconut oil - 1/2 cup unsalted margarine - 2 teaspoons heating powder - 1 teaspoon salt margarine or an olive oil shower

Directions: Crack 6 large eggs into a food processor or blending bowl and mix well. Then add the almond flour or almond supper and the coconut flour. Melt the coconut oil and margarine in the microwave and add it to the blend. Then add the salt and heating powder and blend or mix everything completely. Let it aside for 10-15 minutes so the blend thickens while you preheat your broiler to 350° F. Coat a 9" x 5" heating tin with margarine or an olive oil shower and add your thickened blend to the tin. Pop the tin into the broiler and heat for 40 minutes. Haul the bread out when it turns a brilliant dark colored on top and let it cool on a rack.

Nutrition: Calories: 220 / Carbs: 4 g / Net Carbs: 2.5 g / Fiber: 4 g / Fat: 12 g / Protein: 8 g

25. SAUERKRAUT RYE BREAD

Preparation time: 5 minutes - Cooking time: 3 hours - Servings: 1 loaf

Ingredients: 1 cup sauerkraut – rinsed and drained - 3/4 cup warm water
1 ½ tablespoons molasses - 1 ½ tablespoons butter - 1 ½ tablespoons brown sugar
1 teaspoon caraway seed - 1 ½ teaspoons salt - 1 cup rye flour - 2 cups bread flour
1 ½ teaspoons active dry yeast

Directions: Add all ingredients to the machine pan. Select Basic bread setting.

Nutrition: Calories: 74 / Total fat: 1.8 g (0 g sat. fat) / Carbs: 12 g / Fiber: 1 g / Protein: 1.8 g

26. KETO BLUEBERRY-BANANA LOAF

**Preparation time: 10 minutes - Cooking time: 2 hours 20 minutes
Total Time: 2 hours 30 minutes - Servings: 12 slices**

Ingredients: ½ cup warm water - 1 tablespoon almond milk, unsweetened - 2 eggs, small
8 tablespoons Butter, melted, and unsalted - 3 medium-sized mashed bananas - 0.75 teaspoon stevia extract - 2 cups almond flour - ½ teaspoon salt - 2 teaspoons Baking powder - 1 teaspoon baking soda - 1 cup frozen blueberries

Directions: Prepare the ingredients. Beat the eggs and mash the bananas. Soften the butter in the microwave for 30 seconds. Mix the water and the milk. Put the bananas, eggs, butter, water, and milk in the bread bucket. Add in all dry ingredients except blueberries. Start the bread machine by selecting Quick Bread, then close the lid. After the first kneading, open the lid and add in the blueberries. Close the lid and let the cycle continue until the end. Once cooked, remove the bread from the bucket and let it cool in a cooling rack before slicing. Serve.

Nutrition: Calories: 119 / Calories from fat: 90 / Total Fat: 9 g / Total Carbohydrates: 9 g
Net Carbohydrates: 7 g / Protein: 2 g

27. ANISE ALMOND BREAD

Preparation time: 10 minutes - Cooking time: 3 hours - Servings: 1 loaf

Ingredients: 3/4 cup water - 1 or 1/4 cup egg substitute - 1/4 cup butter or margarine, softened - 1/4 cup sugar - 1/2 teaspoon salt - 3 cups bread flour - 1 teaspoon anise seed 2 teaspoons active dry yeast - 1/2 cup almonds, chopped small

Directions: Add all ingredients to machine pan except almonds. Select Basic bread setting. After prompt, add almonds.

Nutrition: Calories: 78 / Total fats: 4 g (1 g sat. fat) / Carb: 7 g / Fiber: 0 / Protein: 3 g

28. THREE INGREDIENT BUTTERMILK CORNBREAD

Preparation time: 10 Minutes - Cooking time: 20 Minutes - Servings: 8

Ingredients: Vegetable oil as needed - 1 1/2 cups buttermilk - 1 1/2 cups cornmeal 1/2 cup all-purpose flour

Directions: Preheat oven to 450 °F (230 °C). Pour enough oil into a skillet to coat the bottom; place into the oven. Mix buttermilk, cornmeal, and flour together in a bowl until smooth. Remove skillet from oven; pour in buttermilk mixture. Bake in the preheated oven until cornbread is golden brown— 20 to 25 minutes.

Nutrition: Calories: 157 / Total Fat: 2.6 g / Total Carbohydrate: 28.6 g

29. THE BEST CORN BREAD YOU'LL EVER EAT

Preparation time: 5 Minutes - Cooking time: 30 Minutes - Servings: 8

Ingredients: 1 egg - 1 1/3 cups milk - 1/4 cup vegetable oil - 2 cups self-rising corn meal mix 1 (8 ounce) can cream-style corn - 1 cup sour cream

Directions: Heat oven to 425 °F (220 °C). Grease a 9 inch iron skillet. In a large bowl, beat the egg. Add milk, oil, sour cream, cream corn, and cornmeal mix; stir until cornmeal is just dampened. Pour batter into greased skillet. Bake for 25 to 30 minutes, or until knife inserted in center comes out clean.

Nutrition: Calories: 328 / Total Fat: 15.9 g / Total Carbohydrate: 40.8 g / Protein: 6.4 g

30. MACADAMIA NUT BREAD

Preparation time: 10 minutes - Cooking time: 40 minutes - Servings: 6

Ingredients: 5 oz. macadamia nuts - 5 large eggs - ¼ cup coconut flour - ½ teaspoon baking soda - ½ teaspoon apple cider vinegar

Directions: Start by preheating the oven to 350 °F. Blend macadamia nuts in a food processor until it forms a nut butter. Continue blending while adding eggs one by one until well incorporated. Stir in apple cider vinegar, baking soda, and coconut flour. Blend until well mixed and incorporated. Grease a bread pan with cooking spray and spread the batter in a pan. Bake the batter for 40 minutes approximately until golden brown. Slice and serve.

Nutrition: Calories: 248 / Total Fat: 19.3 g / Saturated Fat: 4.8 g / Total Carbs: 3.1 g Fiber 0.6 g / Protein: 7.9 g

31. BULGUR BREAD

Preparation time: 3 hours - Cooking time: 3 hours - Servings: 8

Ingredients: ½ cup bulgur - 1/3 cup boiling water - 1 egg - 1 cup water - 1 tablespoon butter 1 ½ tablespoon milk powder - 1 tablespoon sugar - 2 teaspoons salt - 3 ¼ cups flour - 1 teaspoon dried yeast

Directions: Pour bulgur in boiling water into a small container and cover with a lid. Leave to stand for 30 min. Cut butter into small cubes. Stir the egg with water in a measuring container. The total volume of eggs with water should be 300 ml. Put all the ingredients in the bread maker in the order that is described in the instructions for your bread maker. Bake in the Basic mode, Medium crust.

Nutrition: Carbohydrates 3 g / Fats 3 g / Protein 8.9 g / Calories 255 / Fiber: 1.2 g

32. FRENCH HAM BREAD

Preparation time: 3 hours 30 minutes - Cooking time: 3 hours 30 min - Servings: 8

Ingredients: 3 1/3 cups Almond flour - 1 cup ham - ½ cup milk powder - 1 ½ tablespoons sugar - 1 teaspoon yeast, fresh - 1 teaspoon salt - 1 teaspoon dried basil - 1 1/3 cups water 2 tablespoons olive oil

Directions: Cut ham into cubes of 0.5-1 cm (approximately ¼ inch). Put the ingredients in the bread maker in the following order: water, olive oil, salt, sugar, flour, milk powder, ham, and yeast. Put all the ingredients according to the instructions to your bread maker. Put basil in a dispenser or fill it later at the signal in the container. Turn on the bread machine. After the end of the Baking cycle, leave the bread container in the bread maker to keep warm for 1 hour. Then your delicious bread is ready!

Nutrition: Carbohydrates: 2 g / Fats: 5.5 g / Protein: 11.4 g / Calories: 287 / Fiber: 1 g

33. SOURDOUGH KETO BAGUETTES

Preparation time: 5 minutes - Cooking time: 17 min - Servings: 10

Ingredients: Dry Ingredients: 1/2 cup almond flour (150 g/5.3 oz.) - 1/3 cup phylum husk powder (40 g/1.4 oz.) - 1/2 cup coconut flour (60 g/2.1 oz.) - 1/2 stuffed cup flax supper (75 g/2.6 oz.) - 1 teaspoon preparing pop - 1 teaspoon salt (pink Himalayan or ocean salt)
Wet Ingredients: 6 large egg whites - 2 large eggs - 3/4 cup low-fat buttermilk (180 g/6.5 oz.) full-fat would make them excessively overwhelming and they may not rise - 1/4 cup white wine vinegar or apple juice vinegar (60 ml/2 fl oz.) - 1 cup tepid water (240 ml/8 fl oz.)

Directions: Preheat the broiler to 180 °C/360 °F (fan helped). Use a kitchen scale to gauge every one of the ingredients cautiously. Blend all the dry ingredients in a bowl (almond flour, coconut flour, ground flaxseed, psyllium powder, heating pop, and salt). In a different bowl, blend the eggs, egg whites, and buttermilk. The explanation you shouldn't use just entire eggs is that the bread wouldn't rise with such a large number of egg yolks in. Try not to squander them —use them for making Homemade Mayo, Easy Hollandaise Sauce, or Lemon Curd. For a similar explanation, use low-fat (not full-fat) buttermilk. Add the egg blend and mix them well, using a blender until the mixture is thick. Add vinegar and tepid water and follow procedure until well combined. Don't over-process the mixture. Using a spoon, make 8 ordinary or 16 smaller than usual rolls and place them on a preparing plate fixed with material paper or a non-stick tangle. They will rise, so make a point to leave some space between them. Alternatively, score the loaves slantingly and make 3-4 cuts. Place in the stove and cook for 10 minutes. Then, decrease the temperature to 150 °C/300 °F and heat for another 30-45 minutes (little loaves will set aside because they need less effort to cook). Remove from the stove, let the plate chill off and place the rolls on a rack to chill off to room temperature. Store them at room temperature on the off chance that you intend to use them in the following couple of days or store in the cooler for as long as 3 months. Cooked products that use psyllium consistently result in a marginally wet surface. If necessary, cut the rolls down the middle and place in a toaster or in the broiler before serving. Tip: To spare time, blend all the dry ingredients ahead and store in a zip-lock sack, and add a mark with the number of servings. At the point when fit to be prepared, simply include the wet ingredients!

Nutrition: Calories: 21 / Fat: 4.7 g / Carbs: 44.2 g / Protein: 0 g / Sugars: 5 g

34. TOAST BREAD

Preparation time: 3 ½ hours - Cooking time: 3 ½ hours - Servings: 8

Ingredients: 1 ½ teaspoons yeast - 3 cups almond flour - 2 tablespoons sugar - 1 teaspoon salt 1 ½ tablespoon butter - 1 cup water

Directions: Pour water into the bowl; add salt, sugar, soft butter, flour, and yeast. I add dried tomatoes and paprika. Put it on the Basic program. The crust can be Light or medium.

Nutrition: Carbohydrates 5 g / Fats 2.7 g / Protein 5.2 g / Calories 203 / Fiber 1 g

WHOLE WHEAT BREAD

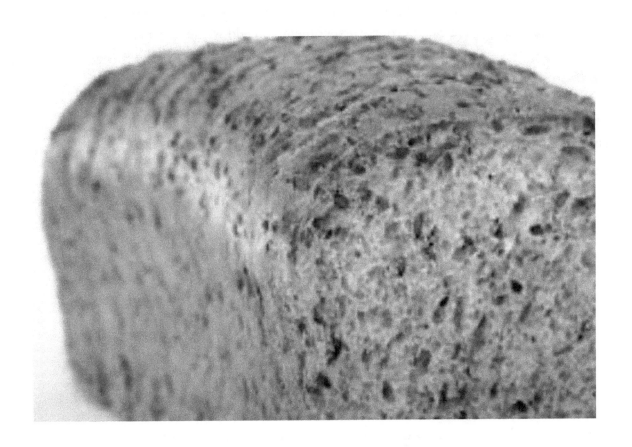

35. BASIC WHOLE WHEAT BREAD

Preparation Time: 9 Minutes - Cooking Time: 4 Hours - Servings: 12 slices

Ingredients: 1 cup lukewarm water - 1 tbsp. Olive oil - 2 cups Whole wheat flour sifted
½ tsp Salt - 1 Tbsp. Soft brown sugar - 2 tbsp. Dried milk powder, skimmed
2 tbsp. Fast-acting, easy-blend dried yeast

Directions: Add the water and olive oil to your machine, followed by half of the flour. Now apply the salt, sugar, dried milk powder, and remaining flour. Make a little well or dip at the top of the flour. Then carefully place the yeast into it, making sure it doesn't come into contact with any liquid. Set the whole meal or whole-wheat setting according to your machine's manual, and alter the crust setting to your particular liking. Once baked, carefully remove the bowl from the machine and remove the loaf, placing it on a wire rack to cool. I prefer not to add any toppings to this particular loaf, but you can, of course, experiment and add whatever you want. Once cool, remove the paddle; and, for the very best results, slice with a serrated bread knife. Enjoy!

Nutrition: Calories: 160 / Carbs: 30.1 g / Fat: 3.1 g / Protein: 5 g

36. HONEY WHOLE-WHEAT BREAD

Preparation Time: 10 Min - Cooking Time: 3 Hours and 40 Min - Servings: 8 slices

Ingredients: 2 cups Water at 90°F–100°F (320°C–370°C) - 2 tbsp. Honey - 1 tbsp. Melted butter, at room temperature - ½ tsp Salt - 2 cups Whole-wheat flour - 1 tbsp. Active dry yeast

Directions: Place the ingredients in your bread machine follow the order of your manufacturer's suggestion. Choose the Whole Wheat program, light or medium crust, and press START. Once baked, let the loaf cool for 10 minutes. Gently wiggle the bucket to remove the loaf. Then transfer it onto a rack to cool. Enjoy!

Nutrition: Calories: 101 / Carbs: 19 g / Fat: 2 g / Protein: 4 g

37. WHOLE WHEAT PEANUT BUTTER AND JELLY BREAD

Preparation Time: 10 Minutes - Cooking Time: 3 Hours - Servings: 12 slices

Ingredients: 2 cups of Water at 90°F–100°F (320°C–370°C) - 2 tbsp. Smooth peanut butter
1 tbsp. Strawberry jelly (or any preferable jelly) - 1 tbsp. Vital wheat gluten - ½ tsp Salt
1 tbsp. Baking soda - ½ tsp Active dry yeast - 1 tbsp. Baking powder - 1 Light brown sugar
2 cups Whole wheat flour

Directions: As you prep the bread machine pan, add the following in this particular order: water, jelly, salt, peanut butter, brown sugar, baking powder, baking soda, gluten, whole wheat flour, and yeast. Choose 1 ½ Pound Loaf, Medium Crust, Wheat cycle, and then START the machine. Once baked, place it on a rack to cool and then serve. Enjoy!

Nutrition: Calories: 230 / Carbs: 39 g / Fat: 6 g / Protein: 9 g

38. BREAD MACHINE EZEKIEL BREAD

Preparation Time: 10 Minutes - Cooking Time: 3 Hours - Servings: 12 slices

Ingredients: ¼ cups Whole wheat flour - 2 cups Bread flour - ¼ cup Spelled flour
1 tbsp. Honey - 1 tbsp. Millet - 1 tbsp. Olive oil - 1 tbsp. Wheat germ - 1 tbsp. Dry kidney beans
1 tbsp. Barley - 1 tbsp. Dry lentils - 1 tbsp. Bread machine yeast - 1 tbsp. Dry black beans
2 cup Water at 90°F (320°C) - ½ tsp Salt

Directions: Soak all beans and grains in separate bowls overnight. Boil the black beans, dry kidney beans for about 1 hour, and then add lentils, millet, and barley. Next, boil for 15 minutes more. Assemble boiled ingredients in a food processor and mix until mashed. Spread water into the bread machine pan, add 2 tbsp. of olive oil and honey, and then add the flour, wheat germ. In one corner, add salt in another one yeast and START the Dough cycle. When the bread machine beeps, add the mash to the dough and press the Whole Wheat cycle. Enjoy!

Nutrition: Calories: 192 / Carbs: 31 g / Fat: 5 g / Protein: 6 g

39. HONEY-OAT-WHEAT BREAD

Preparation Time: 10 Min - Cooking Time: 3 Hours and 45 Min - Servings: 16 slices

Ingredients: Active dry yeast - 2 tbsp. Sugar - 2 cup Water at 1100°F (450°C)
2 cup All-purpose flour - ¼ cup Whole wheat flour - 1 cup Rolled oats - 1 tbsp. Powdered milk
½ tsp Salt - 2 tbsp. Honey - 2 tbsp. Vegetable oil - 1 tbsp. Butter softened - Cooking spray

Directions: Place the following into the pan of a bread machine: yeast, sugar, and water. Let the yeast dissolve and foam for approximately 10 minutes. In the meantime, in a bowl, combine the all-purpose flour, powdered milk, whole wheat flour, salt, and rolled oats. Pour the butter, honey, and vegetable oil into the yeast mixture. Then add the flour mixture on top. Choose the Dough cycle and then push the START button. Let the bread machine fully finish the process, which spans approximately 1 ½ hour. Place the dough into a 9x5-inch loaf pan that's coated with cooking spray. Leave the bread to rise in a warm place for 1 hour. Preheat the oven. Bake for approximately 35 minutes in the warmed oven until the top turns golden brown. Enjoy!

Nutrition: Calories: 281 / Carbs: 45 g / Fat: 9 g / Protein: 6 g

40. BUTTER UP BREAD

Preparation Time: 10 Minutes - Cooking Time: 3 Hours - Servings: 12 slices

Ingredients: 1 cup Bread flour - 2 tbsp. Margarine, melted - 2 tbsp. Buttermilk at 1100°F (450°C) - 1 tbsp. Sugar - 1 tbsp. Active dry yeast - 2 Eggs, at room temperature - ½ tsp Salt

Directions: Prepare the bread machine pan by adding buttermilk, melted margarine, salt, sugar, flour, and yeast in the order specified by your manufacturer. Select Basic/White Setting and press START. Once baked, transfer onto wire racks to cool before slicing. Enjoy!

Nutrition: Calories: 231 / Carbs: 36 g / Fat: 6 g / Protein: 8 g

41. BUTTER HONEY WHEAT BREAD

Preparation Time: 5 Min - Cooking Time: 3 Hours and 45 Min - Servings: 12 slices

Ingredients: 1 tbsp. Buttermilk - 2 tbsp. Butter, melted - 1 tbsp. Honey - 2 cups Bread flour ¼ cup Whole wheat flour - ½ tsp Salt - 1 tbsp. Baking soda - 1 tbsp.[Active dry yeast

Directions: Put all ingredients into the bread machine, by way of recommended by the manufacturer. In my case, liquids always go first. Run the bread machine for a loaf (1½ lbs.) on the Whole Wheat setting. Once the baking process is done, transfer the baked bread to a wire rack and cool before slicing. Enjoy!

Nutrition: Calories: 170 / Carbs: 27 g / Fat: 6 g / Protein: 3 g

42. BUTTERMILK WHEAT BREAD

Preparation Time: 8 Min - Cooking Time: 4 Hours and 30 Min - Servings: 16 slices

Ingredients: 2 tbsp. Buttermilk, at room temperature - 1 cup White sugar - 1 tbsp. Olive oil ½ tsp Salt - 1 tbsp. Baking soda - 2 cup Unbleached white flour - ¼ cup Whole wheat flour Active dry yeast

Directions: In the bread machine pan, measure all ingredients in the order the manufacturer recommends. Set the machine to the Basic White Bread setting and press START. After a few minutes, add more buttermilk if the ingredients don't form a ball. If it's too loose, apply a handful of flour. One baked, let the bread cool on a wire rack before slicing. Enjoy!

Nutrition: Calories: 141 / Carbs: 26 g / Fat: 2.5 g / Protein: 5 g

43. CRACKED FIT AND FAT BREAD

Preparation Time: 5 Min - Cooking Time: 3 Hours and 25 Min - Servings: 16 slices

Ingredients: 1 cup Water - 1 tbsp. Butter softened - 1 tbsp. Brown sugar - ½ tsp Salt ¼ cup Bread flour - 1 cup Whole wheat flour - 1 tbsp. Cracked wheat - 2 tbsp. Active dry yeast

Directions: In the bread machine pan, measure all components according to the manufacturer's suggested order. Choose Basic/White cycle, medium crust, and 2lbs weight of loaf, and then press START. Once baked, allow the bread to cool on a wire rack before slicing. Enjoy!

Nutrition: Calories: 65 / Carbs: 12.4 g / Fat: 1 g / Protein: 2 g

44. CRUNCHY HONEY WHEAT BREAD

Preparation Time: 7 Min - Cooking Time: 3 Hours and 30 Min - Servings: 12 slices

Ingredients: 2 cup Warm water at 1100°F (450°C) - 2 tbsp. Vegetable oil - 1 tbsp. Honey
½ tsp Salt - 1 cup Bread flour - ¼ cup Whole wheat flour - 1 tbsp. Granola - Active dry yeast

Directions: Place the ingredients into the bread machine following the order recommended by the manufacturer. Choose the Whole Wheat setting or the Dough cycle on the machine. Press the START button. Once the machine has finished the whole cycle of baking the bread in the oven, form the dough and add it into a loaf pan that's greased. Let it rise in volume in a warm place until it becomes double its size. Insert into the preheated 350°F (175°C) oven and bake for 35-45 minutes. Enjoy!

Nutrition: Calories: 199 / Carbs: 37 g / Fat: 4.2 g / Protein: 6.2 g

45. EASY HOME BASE WHEAT BREAD

Preparation Time: 10 Min - Cooking Time: 3 Hours and 50 Min - Servings: 12 slices

Ingredients: 2 cups Whole wheat flour - ¼ cup Bread flour - 1 tbsp. Butter softened
1 cup Warm water at 900°F (320°C) - 1 cup Warm milk at 900°F (320°C) - Active dry yeast
2 Egg, at room temperature - ½ tsp Salt - 2 tbsp. Honey

Directions: Add the ingredients into the pan of the bread machine following the order suggested by the manufacturer. Use the Whole Wheat cycle, choose the crust color, weight, and START the machine. Check how the dough is kneading after five minutes pass because you may need to add either one tbsp. of water or one tbsp. of flour-based on consistency. When the bread is complete, cool it on a wire rack before slicing. Enjoy!

Nutrition: Calories: 180 / Carbs: 33 g / Fat: 2 g / Protein: 7 g

46. WHOLE WHEAT YOGURT BREAD

Preparation Time: 10 Min - Cooking Time: 3 Hours and 40 Min - Servings: 12 slices

Ingredients: 1 tbsp. Ground nutmeg (optional) - 2 cups Water - 2 tbsp. Butter, melted
¼ cup Plain yogurt - 2 tbsp. Dry milk - 2 tbsp. Honey - 1 tbsp. Active dry yeast
1 cup Whole wheat flour - 1 cup Bread flour - 2 tbsp. Ground cinnamon - ½ tsp Salt

Directions: Begin by pouring ingredients into the bread pan in the instruction your manufacturer endorses. In my case, liquids always go first. So, I begin with water, yogurt, butter, honey, sieve flour, dry milk, add salt, ground cinnamon, and yeast in different corners of the pan. Select the Whole grain setting, light or medium crust, and press START. When ready, allow it to cool and then serve. Enjoy!

Nutrition: Calories: 158 / Carbs: 20 g / Fat: 5 g / Protein: 6 g

CHEESE BREAD

47. CHEESE BUTTERMILK BREAD

Preparation Time: 5 Minutes - Cooking Time: 2 Hours - Servings: 10

Ingredients: 1 1/8 cups Buttermilk - 1 ½ tsp. - Active dry yeast - ¾ cup. Cheddar cheese shredded - 1 ½ tsp. Sugar - 3 cups. Bread flour - 1 1/2 tsp. Salt

Directions: Place all ingredients into the bread machine pan based on the bread machine manufacturer instructions. Select basic bread setting, then select light/medium crust and start. Once the loaf is done, remove the loaf pan from the machine. Allow it to cool for 10 minutes. Slice and serve.

Nutrition: Calories 182 / Carbs 30 g / Fat 3.4 g / Protein 6.8 g

48. DELICIOUS ITALIAN CHEESE BREAD

Preparation Time: 5 Minutes - Cooking Time: 2 Hours - Servings: 10

Ingredients: 2 tsp. Active dry yeast – 2 tbsp. Brown sugar – 2 tbsp. Parmesan cheese grated 1 tsp. Ground black pepper – 2 tsp. Italian seasoning – ½ cup Pepper jack cheese, shredded 3 cups Bread flour - 1 ¼ cups Warm water - 1 ½ tsp Salt

Directions: First, add all ingredients to the bread machine pan. Select a basic setting, then select a light/medium crust and start. Once the loaf is done, remove the loaf pan from the machine. Allow it to cool for 10 minutes. Slice and serve.

Nutrition: Calories 163 / Carbs 31.1 g / Fat 1.8 g / Protein 5.3 g

49. BEER CHEESE BREAD

Preparation Time: 5 Minutes - Cooking Time: 2 Hours - Servings: 10

Ingredients: 4 oz Monterey Jack cheese, shredded - 4 oz American cheese, shredded 10 oz Beer 1 tbsp. Butter - 1 tbsp. Sugar – 3 cups Bread flour – 1 packet Active dry yeast 1 ½ tsp. Salt

Directions: Place the ingredients into the pan of the bread machine. Select the basic setting, then select a light crust and start. Once the loaf is done, remove the loaf pan from the machine. Allow it to cool for 10 minutes. Slice and serve.

Nutrition: Calories 245 / Carbs 32.1 g / Fat 7.8 g / Protein 9.2 g

50. MOIST CHEDDAR CHEESE BREAD

Preparation Time: 5 Minutes - Cooking Time: 3 Hours and 45 Min - Servings: 10

Ingredients: Milk – 1 cup / Butter – ½ cup, melted / All-purpose flour – 3 cups
Cheddar cheese – 2 cups, shredded / Garlic powder – ½ tsp. / Kosher salt 2 tsp.
Sugar – 1 tbsp. / Active dry yeast – 1 ¼ oz.

Directions: Add milk and butter into the bread pan. Add remaining ingredients except for yeast to the bread pan. Make a narrow hole into the flour with your finger and add yeast to the punch. Make sure yeast will not be mixed with any liquids. Select the basic setting, then select a light crust and start. Once the loaf is done, remove the loaf pan from the machine. Allow it to cool for 10 minutes. Slice and serve.

Nutrition: Calories 337 / Carbs 32.8 g / Fat 17.7 g / Protein 11.8 g

51. CHEESE PEPPERONI BREAD

Preparation Time: 5 Minutes - Cooking Time: 2 Hours - Servings: 10

Ingredients: Pepperoni – 2/3 cup, diced / Active dry yeast – 1 ½ tsp.
Bread flour – 3 ¼ cups. / Dried oregano – 1 ½ tsp. / Garlic salt – 1 ½ tsp. / Sugar – 2 tbsp.
Mozzarella cheese – 1/3 cup., shredded / Warm water – 1 cup+2 tbsp.

Directions: Add all ingredients except for pepperoni into the bread machine pan. Select basic setting, then selects medium crust and press start. Add pepperoni just before the final kneading cycle. Once the loaf is done, remove the loaf pan from the machine. Allow it to cool for 10 minutes. Slice and serve.

Nutrition: Calories 176 / Carbs 34.5 g / Fat 1.5 g / Protein 5.7 g

52. GLUTEN-FREE CHEESY BREAD

Preparation Time: 5 Minutes - Cooking Time: 4 Hours - Servings: 10

Ingredients: Eggs – 3 / Olive oil – 2 tbsp. / Water – 1 ½ cups. / Active dry yeast – 2 ¼ tsp.
White rice flour – 2 cups. / Brown rice flour – 1 cup. / Milk powder – ¼ cup. / Sugar – 2 tbsp.
Poppy seeds – 1 tbsp. / Xanthan gum – 3 ½ tsp. / Cheddar cheese – 1 ½ cups., shredded
Salt – 1 tsp.

Directions: In a bowl, mix eggs, water, and oil and pour it into the bread machine pan. In a large bowl, mix the other ingredients and pour over wet ingredient mixture into the bread pan. Select the whole wheat setting, then select light/medium crust and start. Once the loaf is done, remove the loaf pan from the machine. Allow it to cool for 10 minutes. Slice and serve.

Nutrition: Calories 317 / Carbs 43.6 g / Fat 11 g / Protein 10.6 g

53. GARLIC PARMESAN BREAD

Preparation Time: 5 Minutes - Cooking Time: 3 Hours and 45 Min - Servings: 10

Ingredients: Active dry yeast – ¼ oz. / Sugar– 3 tbsp. / Kosher salt – 2 tsp. Dried oregano – 1 tsp. / Dried basil – 1 tsp. / Garlic powder – ½ tsp. Parmesan cheese – ½ cup grated / All-purpose flour – 3 ½ cups / Garlic – 1 tbsp., minced Butter – ¼ cup, melted / Olive oil – 1/3 cup / Water – 1 1/3 cups

Directions: Add water, oil, butter, and garlic into the bread pan. Add remaining ingredients except for yeast to the bread pan. Make a small hole in the flour with your finger and add yeast to the spot. Make sure yeast will not be mixed with any liquids. Select the basic setting, then selects a light crust and start. Once the loaf is done, remove the loaf pan from the machine. Allow it to cool for 10 minutes. Slice and serve.

Nutrition: Calories 335 / Carbs 37.7 g / Fat 15.4 g / Protein 9.7 g

54. CHEESE JALAPENO BREAD

Preparation Time: 5 Minutes - Cooking Time: 2 Hours - Servings: 10

Ingredients: Monterey jack cheese – ¼ cup shredded / Active dry yeast – 2 tsp. Butter – 1 ½ tbsp. / Sugar – 1 ½ tbsp. / Milk – 3 tbsp. / Flour – 3 cups. / Water – 1 cup. Jalapeno pepper – 1, minced / Salt – 1 ½ tsp.

Directions: Begin by adding all fixings to the bread machine pan according to the bread machine manufacturer instructions. Select basic bread setting, then select light/medium crust and start. Once the loaf is done, remove the loaf pan from the machine. Allow it to cool for 10 minutes. Slice and serve.

Nutrition: Calories 174 / Carbs 31.1 g / Fat 3.1 g / Protein 5.1 g

55. ITALIAN HERB CHEESE BREAD

Preparation Time: 5 Minutes - Cooking Time: 3 Hours - Servings: 10

Ingredients: Yeast – 1 ½ tsp. / Italian herb seasoning – 1 tbsp. / Brown sugar – 2 tbsp. Cheddar cheese – 1 cup., shredded / Bread flour – 3 cups. / Butter – 4 tbsp. / Warm milk 1 ¼ cups. / Salt – 2 tsp.

Directions: Add milk into the bread pan. Add remaining ingredients except for yeast to the bread pan. Make a small hole into the flour with your finger and add yeast to the spot. Make sure yeast will not be mixed with any liquids. Select a basic setting, then selects a light crust and start. Once the loaf is done, remove the loaf pan from the machine. Allow it to cool for 10 minutes. Slice and serve.

Nutrition: Calories 247 / Carbs 32.3 g / Fat 9.4 g / Protein 8 g

56. CHEDDAR CHEESE BASIL BREAD

Preparation Time: 10 Minutes - Cooking Time: 25 Minutes - Servings: 8

Ingredients: 1 cup milk - One tablespoon melted butter cooled - One tablespoon sugar One teaspoon dried basil - ¾ cup (3 ounces) shredded sharp Cheddar cheese ¾ teaspoon salt cups white bread flour - 1½ teaspoons active dry yeast

Directions: Preparing the Ingredients. Place the ingredients in your Zojirushi bread machine. Select the Bake cycle. Program the machine for Regular Basic, choose light or medium crust, and then press Start. If the loaf is done, remove the bucket from the machine. Let the loaf cool for 5 minutes. Softly shake the canister to remove the loaf and put it out onto a rack to cool.

Nutrition: Calories 174 / Carbs 31.1 g / Fat 3.1 g / Protein 5.1 g

57. HERB AND PARMESAN CHEESE LOAF

Preparation Time: 10 Minutes - Cooking Time: 25 Minutes - Servings: 8

Ingredients: cups + 2 tbsp. all-purpose flour - 1 cup of water - 2 tbsp. oil - 1 tbsp. sugar 2 tbsp. milk - 1 tbsp. instant yeast - 1 tsp. garlic powder - 2 tbsp. parmesan cheese 1 tbsp. fresh basil - 1 tbsp. fresh oregano - 1 tbsp. fresh chives or rosemary

Directions: Preparing the Ingredients. Place all fixings in the bread pan in the liquid-cheese and herb-dry-yeast layering. Put the pan in the Zojirushi bread machine. Select the Bake cycle. Choose Regular Basic Setting. Press start and wait until the loaf is cooked. The machine will start the keep warm mode after the bread is complete. Just allow it to stay in that mode for about 10 minutes before unplugging. Remove the pan and wait for it to cool down for about 10 minutes.

Nutrition: Calories 174 / Carbs 31.1 g / Fat 3.1 g / Protein 5.1 g

58. OLIVE CHEESE BREAD

Preparation Time: 10 Minutes - Cooking Time: 25 Minutes - Servings: 8

Ingredients: 1 cup milk - 1½ tablespoons melted butter, cooled - One teaspoon minced garlic 1½ tablespoons sugar - One teaspoon salt - 2 cups white bread flour - ¾ cup (3 ounces) shredded Swiss cheese - One teaspoon bread machine or instant yeast - 1/3 cup chopped black olives

Directions: Preparing the Ingredients. Place the ingredients in your Zojirushi bread machine, tossing the flour with the cheese first. Program the machine for Regular Basic, choose light or medium crust, and press Start. Next, when the loaf is done, you may remove the bucket from the machine. Let the loaf cool for 5 minutes. Mildly shake the pot to eliminate the loaf and turn it out onto a rack to cool.

Nutrition: Calories 174 / Carbs 31.1 g / Fat 3.1 g / Protein 5.1 g

59. BEER AND CHEESE BREAD

Preparation Time: 10 Minutes - Cooking Time: 25 Minutes - Servings: 8

Ingredients: 3 cups bread or all-purpose flour - 1 tbsp. instant yeast - 1 tsp. salt 1 tbsp. sugar 1 1/2 cup beer at room temperature - 1/2 cup shredded Monterey cheese - 1/2 cup shredded Edam cheese

Directions: Place all elements, except cheeses, in the bread pan in the liquid-dry-yeast layering. Put the pan in the Zojirushi bread machine. Select the Bake cycle. Choose Regular Basic Setting. Press Start. When the kneading process is about to end, add the cheese. Wait until the loaf is cooked. The machine will start the keep warm mode after the bread is complete. Do not forget to let it stay in that mode for about 10 minutes before unplugging. Lastly, remove the pan and let it cool down for about 10 minutes.

Nutrition: Calories 174 / Carbs 31.1 g / Fat 3.1 g / Protein 5.1 g

60. BLUE CHEESE ONION BREAD

Preparation Time: 10 Minutes - Cooking Time: 25 Minutes - Servings: 8

Ingredients: 1¼ cup water, at 80°F to 90°F - One egg, at room temperature
One tablespoon melted butter cooled - ¼ cup powdered skim milk - One tablespoon sugar
¾ teaspoon salt - ½ cup (2 ounces) crumbled blue cheese - One tablespoon dried onion flake
3 cups white bread flour - ¼ cup instant mashed potato flakes - One teaspoon bread machine or active dry yeast

Directions: Preparing the Ingredients. Place the ingredients in your Zojirushi bread machine. Program the machine for Regular Basic, select light or medium crust, and press Start. Remove the bucket from the machine. Let the loaf cool for 5 minutes. Gently shake the container to remove the loaf and turn it out onto a rack to cool.

Nutrition: Calories 174 / Carbs 31.1 g / Fat 3.1 g / Protein 5.1 g

61. CHEESE LOAF

Preparation Time: 10 Minutes - Cooking Time: 25 Minutes - Servings: 8

Ingredients: 1/4 cups flour - 1 tsp. instant yeast - 1 3/4 cups water - 1 tbsp. sugar
1 1/2 cup shredded cheddar cheese - 1 tbsp. parmesan cheese - 1 tsp. mustard
1 tsp. paprika - 1 tbsp. minced white onion - 1/3 cup butter

Directions: Begin through placing all ingredients in the bread pan in the liquid-dry-yeast layering. Put the pan in the Zojirushi bread machine. Select the Bake cycle. Choose Regular Basic Setting and light crust. Press start and wait until the loaf is cooked. The machine will start the keep warm mode after the bread is complete. For about 10 minutes, let the bread stay for 10 minutes in that mode before unplugging. You may now want to remove the pan and let it cool down for about 10 minutes.

Nutrition: Calories 174 / Carbs 31.1 g / Fat 3.1 g / Protein 5.1 g

SPICE AND HERB BREAD

62. HERBAL GARLIC CREAM CHEESE DELIGHT

Preparation Time: 5 min - Cooking Time: 2 hours and 45 min - Servings: 8 slices

Ingredients: 1/3 cup water at 80 degrees F - 1/3 cup herb and garlic cream cheese mix, at room temp - 1 whole egg, beaten, at room temp - 4 teaspoons melted butter, cooled 1 tablespoon sugar - 2/3 teaspoon salt - 2 cups white bread flour - 1 teaspoon instant yeast

Directions: Add all of the ingredients to your bread machine, carefully following the instructions of the manufacturer. Set the program of your bread machine to Basic/White Bread and set crust type to Medium. Wait until the cycle completes. Once the loaf is ready, take the bucket out and let the loaf cool for 5 minutes. Gently shake the bucket to remove the loaf.

Nutrition: Total Carbs: 27 g / Fiber: 2 g / Protein: 5 g / Fat: 6 g / Calories: 182

63. CUMIN TOSSED FANCY BREAD

Preparation Time: 5 min - Cooking Time: 3 hours and 15 min - Servings: 16 slices

Ingredients: 5 1/3 cups wheat flour - 1½ teaspoons salt - 1½ tablespoons sugar - 1 tablespoon dry yeast - 1¾ cups water - 2 tablespoons cumin - 3 tablespoons sunflower oil

Directions: Add warm water to the bread machine bucket. Add salt, sugar, and sunflower oil. Sift in wheat flour and add yeast. Set the program of your bread machine to French bread and set crust type to Medium. Once the maker beeps, add cumin. Wait until the cycle completes. Once the loaf is ready, take the bucket out and let the loaf cool for 5 minutes. Gently shake the bucket to remove the loaf.

Nutrition: Total Carbs: 67 g / Fiber: 2 g / Protein: 9.5 g / Fat: 7 g / Calories: 368

64. POTATO ROSEMARY LOAF

Preparation Time: 5 min - Cooking Time: 3 hours and 25 min - Servings: 20 slices

Ingredients: 4 cups wheat flour - 1 tablespoon sugar - 1 tablespoon sunflower oil 1½ teaspoons salt - 1½ cups water - 1 teaspoon dry yeast - 1 cup mashed potatoes, ground through a sieve - crushed rosemary to taste

Directions: Add flour, salt, and sugar to the bread maker bucket and attach mixing paddle. Add sunflower oil and water. Put in yeast as directed. Set the program of your bread machine to Bread with Filling mode and set crust type to Medium. Once the bread maker beeps and signals to add more ingredients, open lid, add mashed potatoes, and chopped rosemary. Wait until the cycle completes. Once the loaf is ready, take the bucket out and let the loaf cool for 5 minutes. Gently shake the bucket to remove the loaf.

Nutrition: Total Carbs: 54 g / Fiber: 1 g / Protein: 8 g / Fat: 3 g / Calories: 276

65. DELICIOUS HONEY LAVENDER BREAD

Preparation Time: 10 min - Cooking Time: 3 hours and 25 min - Servings: 16 slices

Ingredients: 1½ cups wheat flour - 2 1/3 cups whole meal flour - 1 teaspoon fresh yeast 1½ cups water - 1 teaspoon lavender - 1½ tablespoons honey - 1 teaspoon salt

Directions: Sift both types of flour in a bowl and mix. Add all of the ingredients to your bread machine, carefully following the instructions of the manufacturer. Set the program of your bread machine to Basic/White Bread and set crust type to Medium. Wait until the cycle completes. Once the loaf is ready, take the bucket out and let the loaf cool for 5 minutes. Gently shake the bucket to remove the loaf.

Nutrition: Total Carbs: 46 g / Fiber: 1 g / Protein: 7.5 g / Fat: 1.5 g / Calories: 226

66. INSPIRING CINNAMON BREAD

Preparation Time: 15 min - Cooking Time: 2 hours and 15 min - Servings: 8 slices

Ingredients: 2/3 cup milk at 80 degrees F - 1 whole egg, beaten - 3 tablespoons melted butter, cooled - 1/3 cup sugar - 1/3 teaspoon salt - 1 teaspoon ground cinnamon - 2 cups white bread flour - 1 1/3 teaspoons active dry yeast

Directions: Add all of the ingredients to your bread machine, carefully following the instructions of the manufacturer. Set the program of your bread machine to Basic/White Bread and set crust type to Medium. Wait until the cycle completes. Once the loaf is ready, take the bucket out and let the loaf cool for 5 minutes. Remove the loaf

Nutrition: Total Carbs: 34 g / Fiber: 1 g / Protein: 5 g / Fat: 5 g / Calories: 198

67. LAVENDER BUTTERMILK BREAD

Preparation time: 10 minutes - Cooking time: 3 hours - Servings: 14

Ingredients: ½ cup water - 7/8 cup buttermilk - 1/4 cup olive oil - 3 Tablespoon finely chopped fresh lavender leaves - 1 ¼ teaspoon finely chopped fresh lavender flowers Grated zest of 1 lemon - 4 cups bread flour - 2 teaspoon salt - 2 3/4 teasp. bread machine yeast

Directions: Add each ingredient to the bread machine in the order and at the temperature recommended by your bread machine manufacturer. Close the lid, select the basic bread, medium crust setting on your bread machine and press start. When the bread machine has finished baking, remove the bread and put it on a cooling rack.

Nutrition: Carbs: 27 g / Fat: 5 g / Protein: 2 g / Calories: 170

68. CAJUN BREAD

Preparation time: 10 minutes - Cooking time: 2 hours 10 minutes - Servings: 14

Ingredients: ½ cup water - ¼ cup chopped onion - ¼ cup chopped green bell pepper
2 teaspoon finely chopped garlic - 2 teaspoon soft butter - 2 cups bread flour
1 Tablespoon sugar - 1 teaspoon Cajun - ½ teaspoon salt - 1 teaspoon active dry yeast

Directions : Add each ingredient to the bread machine in the order and at the temperature recommended by your bread machine manufacturer. Close the lid, select the basic bread, medium crust setting on your bread machine and press start. When the bread machine has finished baking, remove the bread and put it on a cooling rack.

Nutrition: Carbs: 23 g / Fat: 4 g / Protein: 5 g / Calories: 150

69. TURMERIC BREAD

Preparation time: 5 minutes - Cooking time: 3 hours - Servings: 14

Ingredients: 1 teaspoon dried yeast - 4 cups strong white flour - 1 teaspoon turmeric powder
2 teaspoon beetroot powder - 2 Tablespoon olive oil - 1.5 teaspoon salt - 1 teaspoon chili flakes
1 3/8 water

Directions: Add each ingredient to the bread machine in the order and at the temperature recommended by your bread machine manufacturer. Close the lid, select the basic bread, medium crust setting on your bread machine and press start. When the bread machine has finished baking, remove the bread and put it on a cooling rack.

Nutrition: Carbs: 24 g / Fat: 3 g / Protein: 2 g / Calories: 129

70. ROSEMARY CRANBERRY PECAN BREAD

Preparation time: 30 minutes - Cooking time: 3 hours - Servings: 14

Ingredients: 1 1/3 cups water, plus - 2 Tablespoon water - 2 Tablespoon butter
2 teaspoon salt - 4 cups bread flour - 3/4 cup dried sweetened cranberries - 3/4 cup toasted chopped pecans - 2 Tablespoon non-fat powdered milk - ¼ cup sugar - 2 teaspoon yeast

Directions: Add each ingredient to the bread machine in the order and at the temperature recommended by your bread machine manufacturer. Close the lid, select the basic bread, medium crust setting on your bread machine and press start. When the bread machine has finished baking, remove the bread and put it on a cooling rack.

Nutrition: Carbs: 18 g / Fat: 5 g / Protein: 9 g / Calories: 120

71. SESAME FRENCH BREAD

Preparation time: 20 minutes - Cooking time: 3 hours 15 minutes - Servings: 14

Ingredients: 7/8 cup water - 1 Tablespoon butter, softened - 3 cups bread flour - 2 teaspoon sugar - 1 teaspoon salt - 2 teaspoon yeast - 2 Tablespoon sesame seeds toasted

Directions: Add each ingredient to the bread machine in the order and at the temperature recommended by your bread machine manufacturer. Close the lid, select the French bread, medium crust setting on your bread machine and press start. When the bread machine has finished baking, remove the bread and put it on a cooling rack.

Nutrition: Carbs: 28 g / Fat: 3 g / Protein: 6 g / Calories: 180

72. HERB BREAD

Preparation Time: 1 hour 20 minutes - Cooking Time: 50 minutes (20+30 minutes) Servings: 1 loaf

Ingredients: 3/4 to 7/8 cup milk - 1 tablespoon Sugar - 1 teaspoon Salt - 2 tablespoon Butter or margarine - 1/3 cup chopped onion - 2 cups bread flour - 1/2 teaspoon Dried dill 1/2 teaspoon Dried basil - 1/2 teaspoon Dried rosemary - 11/2 teaspoon Active dry yeast

Directions: Place all the Ingredients in the bread pan. Select medium crus then the rapid bake cycle. Press starts. After 5-10 minutes, observe the dough as it kneads, if you hear straining sounds in your machine or if the dough appears stiff and dry, add 1 tablespoon Liquid at a time until the dough becomes smooth, pliable, soft, and slightly tacky to the touch. Remove the bread from the pan after baking. Place on rack and allow to cool for 1 hour before slicing.

Nutrition: Calories: 65 / Fat: 0 g / Carbohydrates: 13 g / Protein: 2 g

73. ROSEMARY WHITE BREAD

Preparation Time: 2 hours 10 min - Cooking Time: 50 minutes - Servings: 1 loaf

Ingredients: ¾ cup + 1 tablespoon water at 80 degrees F - 1 2/3 tablespoons melted butter, cooled - 2 teaspoons sugar - 1 teaspoon salt - 1 tablespoon fresh rosemary, chopped 2 cups white bread flour - 1 1/3 teaspoons instant yeast

Directions: Add all of the ingredients to your bread machine, carefully following the instructions of the manufacturer. Set the program of your bread machine to Basic/White Bread and set crust type to Medium. Press START. Wait until the cycle completes. Once the loaf is ready, take the bucket out and let the loaf cool for 5 minutes. Gently shake the bucket to remove the loaf. Transfer to a cooling rack, slice, and serve.

Nutrition: Calories: 142 / Fat: 3 g / Carbohydrates: 25 g / Protein: 4 g / Fiber: 1 g

74. ORIGINAL ITALIAN HERB BREAD

Preparation Time: 2 hours 40 min - Cooking Time: 50 minutes - Servings: 2 loaves

Ingredients: 1 cup water at 80 degrees F - ½ cup olive brine - 1½ tablespoons butter
2 tablespoons sugar - 2 teaspoons salt - 5 1/3 cups flour - 2 teaspoons bread machine yeast
20 olives, black/green - 1½ teaspoons Italian herbs

Directions: Cut olives into slices. Add all of the ingredients to your bread machine (except olives), carefully following the instructions of the manufacturer. Set the program of your bread machine to French bread and set crust type to Medium. Press START. Once the maker beeps, add olives. Wait until the cycle completes. Once the loaf is ready, take the bucket out and let the loaf cool for 5 minutes. Gently shake the bucket to remove the loaf. Transfer to a cooling rack, slice, and serve.

Nutrition: Calories: 386 / Fat: 7 g / Carbohydrates: 71 g / Protein: 10 g / Fiber: 1 g

75. LOVELY AROMATIC LAVENDER BREAD

Preparation Time: 2 hours 10 min - Cooking Time: 50 minutes - Servings: 1 loaf

Ingredients: ¾ cup milk at 80 degrees F - 1 tablespoon melted butter, cooled - 1 tablespoon sugar - ¾ teaspoon salt - 1 teaspoon fresh lavender flower, chopped - ¼ teaspoon lemon zest
¼ teaspoon fresh thyme, chopped - 2 cups white bread flour - ¾ teaspoon instant yeast

Directions: Add all of the ingredients to your bread machine Set the program of your bread machine to Basic/White Bread and set crust type to Medium. Press START. Wait until the cycle completes. Once the loaf is ready, take the bucket out and let the loaf cool for 5 minutes. Gently shake the bucket to remove the loaf. Transfer to a cooling rack, slice, and serve.

Nutrition: Calories: 144 / Fat: 2 g / Carbohydrates: 27 g / Protein: 4 g / Fiber: 1 g

76. OREGANO MOZZA-CHEESE BREAD

Preparation Time: 2 hours 50 min - Cooking Time: 50 minutes - Servings: 2 loaves

Ingredients: 1 cup (milk + egg) mixture - ½ cup mozzarella cheese - 2¼ cups flour
¾ cup whole grain flour - 2 tablespoons sugar - 1 teaspoon salt - 2 teaspoons oregano
1½ teaspoons dry yeast

Directions: Add all of the ingredients to your bread machine Set the program of your bread machine to Basic/White Bread and set crust type to Dark. Press START. Wait until the cycle completes. Once the loaf is ready, take the bucket out and let the loaf cool for 5 minutes. Gently shake the bucket to remove the loaf. Transfer to a cooling rack, slice, and serve.

Nutrition: Calories: 209 / Fat: 2.1 g / Carbohydrates: 40 g / Protein: 7.7 g / Fiber: 1 g

77. GARLIC BREAD

Preparation Time: 2 hours 30 min - Cooking Time: 40 minutes - Servings: 1 loaf

Ingredients: 1 3/8 cups water - 2 tablespoons olive oil - 1 teaspoon minced garlic - 2 cups bread flour - 2 tablespoons white sugar - 2 teaspoons salt - 1/4 cup grated Parmesan cheese 1 teaspoon dried basil - 1 teaspoon garlic powder - 2 tablespoons chopped fresh chives 1 teaspoon coarsely ground black pepper - 1/2 teaspoons bread machine yeast

Directions: Follow the order of putting the ingredients into the pan of the bread machine recommended by the manufacturer.Choose the Basic or the White Bread cycle on the machine and press the Start button.

Nutrition: Calories: 175 / Total Carbohydrate: 29.7 g / Cholesterol: 1 mg / Total Fat: 3.7 g Protein: 5.2 g / Sodium: 332 mg

78. ROSEMARY BREAD

Preparation Time: 2 hours 40 min - Cooking Time: 25- 30 minutes - Servings: 1 loaf

Ingredients: 1 cup water - 2 tablespoons olive oil - 1 1/2 teaspoons white sugar 1 1/2 teaspoons salt - 1/4 teaspoon Italian seasoning - 1/4 teaspoon ground black pepper 1 tablespoon dried rosemary - 1/2 cups bread flour - 1 1/2 teaspoons active dry yeast

Directions: Into the bread machine pan, put the ingredients following the order recommended by manufacturer. Use the white bread cycle and then push the Start button.

Nutrition: Calories: 137 / Total Carbohydrate: 21.6 g / Cholesterol: 0 mg / Total Fat: 3.9 g Protein: 3.6 g / Sodium: 292 mg

79. SAFFRON TOMATO BREAD

Preparation Time: 3 hours 30 minutes - Cooking Time: 15 minutes - Servings: 10

Ingredients: 1 teaspoon bread machine yeast - 2½ cups wheat bread machine flour 1 Tablespoon panifarin - 1½ teaspoon kosher salt - 1½ Tablespoon white sugar - 1 Tablespoon extra-virgin olive oil - 1 Tablespoon tomatoes, dried and chopped - 1 Tablespoon tomato paste ½ cup firm cheese (cubes) - ½ cup feta cheese - 1 pinch saffron - 1½ cups serum

Directions: Five minutes before cooking, pour in dried tomatoes and 1 tablespoon of olive oil. Add the tomato paste and mix. Place all the dry and liquid ingredients, except additives, in the pan and follow the instructions for your bread machine. Pay particular attention to measuring the ingredients. Use a measuring cup, measuring spoon, and kitchen scales to do so. Set the baking program to BASIC and the crust type to MEDIUM. Add the additives after the beep or place them in the dispenser of the bread machine. Shake the loaf out of the pan. If necessary, use a spatula. Wrap the bread with a kitchen towel and set it aside for an hour. Otherwise, you can cool it on a wire rack.

Nutrition: Calories: 260 / Total Carbohydrate: 35.5 g / Cholesterol: 20 g / Total Fat: 9.2 g Protein: 8.9 g / Sodium: 611 mg / Sugar: 5.2 g

80. CRACKED BLACK PEPPER BREAD

Preparation Time: 3 hours 30 minutes - Cooking Time: 15 minutes - Servings: 8

Ingredients: ¾ cup water, at 80°F to 90°F - 1 tablespoon melted butter, cooled
1 tablespoon sugar - ¾ teaspoon salt - 2 tablespoons skim milk powder - 1 tablespoon minced chives - ½ teaspoon garlic powder - ½ teaspoon cracked black pepper - 2 cups white bread flour
¾ teaspoon bread machine or instant yeast

Directions: Place the ingredients in your bread machine as recommended by the manufacturer. Program the machine for Basic/White bread, select light or medium crust, and press Start. When the loaf is done, remove the bucket from the machine. Let the loaf cool for 5 minutes. Gently shake the bucket to remove the loaf, and turn it out onto a rack to cool.

Nutrition: Calories: 141 / Total Carbohydrate: 27 g / Total Fat: 2 g / Protein: 4 g
Sodium: 215 mg / Fiber: 1 g

81. SPICY CAJUN BREAD

Preparation Time: 2 hours - Cooking Time: 15 minutes - Servings: 8

Ingredients: ¾ cup water, at 80°F to 90°F - 1 tablespoon melted butter, cooled
2 teaspoons tomato paste - 1 tablespoon sugar - 1 teaspoon salt - 2 tablespoons skim milk powder - ½ tablespoon Cajun seasoning - 1/8 Teaspoon onion powder - 2 cups white bread flour - 1 teaspoon bread machine or instant yeast

Directions: Place the ingredients in your bread machine as recommended by the manufacturer. Program the machine for Basic/White bread, select light or medium crust, and press Start. When the loaf is done, remove the bucket from the machine. Let the loaf cool for 5 minutes. Gently shake the bucket to remove the loaf, and turn it out onto a rack to cool.

Nutrition: Calories: 141 / Total Carbohydrate: 27 g / Total Fat: 2 g / Protein: 4 g
Sodium: 215 mg / Fiber: 1 g

82. ANISE LEMON BREAD

Preparation Time: 2 hours - Cooking Time: 15 minutes - Servings: 8

Ingredients: 2/3 Cup water, at 80°F to 90°F - 1 egg, at room temperature - 2 2/3 tablespoons butter, melted and cooled - 2 2/3 tablespoons honey - 1/3 Teaspoon salt - 2/3 Teaspoon anise seed - 2/3Teaspoon lemon zest - 2 cups white bread flour - 1 1/3 teaspoons bread machine or instant yeast

Directions: Place the ingredients in your bread machine as recommended by the manufacturer. Program the machine for Basic/White bread, select light or medium crust, and press Start. When the loaf is done, remove the bucket from the machine. Let the loaf cool for 5 minutes. Gently shake the bucket to remove the loaf, and turn it out onto a rack to cool.

Nutrition: Calories: 158 / Total Carbohydrate: 27 g / Total Fat: 5 g / Protein: 4 g
Sodium: 131 mg / Fiber: 1 g

83. CARDAMON BREAD

Preparation Time: 2 hours - Cooking Time: 15 minutes - Servings: 8

Ingredients: ½ cup milk, at 80°F to 90°F - 1 egg, at room temperature - 1 teaspoon melted butter, cooled - Teaspoons honey - 2/3 Teaspoon salt - 2/3 Teaspoon ground cardamom 2 cups white bread flour - ¾ teaspoon bread machine or instant yeast

Directions: Place the ingredients in your bread machine as recommended by the manufacturer. Program the machine for Basic/White bread, select light or medium crust, and press Start. When the loaf is done, remove the bucket from the machine. Let the loaf cool for 5 minutes. Gently shake the bucket to remove the loaf, and turn it out onto a rack to cool.

Nutrition: Calories: 149 / Total Carbohydrate: 29 g / Total Fat: 2g / Protein: 5 g Sodium: 211 mg / Fiber: 1 g

VEGETABLE BREAD

84. CAULIFLOWER BREAD

Preparation time: 10 minutes - Cooking time: 54 minutes - Servings: 8

Ingredients: 3 cup cauliflower rice - 10 large egg - 1/4 tsp. cream of tartar
1 1/4 cup coconut flour - 1 1/2 tbsp. gluten-free baking powder - 1 tsp. sea salt - 6 tbsp. butter
6 cloves garlic (minced) - 1 tbsp. fresh rosemary (chopped) - 1 tbsp. fresh parsley (chopped)

Directions: Start by preheating the oven to 350 degrees F and layer a loaf pan with parchment paper. Place the cauliflower rice in a large bowl and cover it with a plastic sheet. Cook the rice in the microwave for 4 minutes. During this time, beat egg whites with cream of tartar in a bowl until it forms peaks. Whisk coconut flour with egg yolks, salt, baking powder, garlic, and melted butter in a separate bowl. Stir in ¼ egg whites and blend the mixture in a food processor until incorporated. Place the cauliflower rice in a kitchen towel and squeeze to absorb moisture from the rice. Add the cauliflower rice to the food processor and pulse until well mixed. Fold in rosemary and parsley. Spread the cauliflower batter in a baking pan lined with parchment paper. Bake the batter for 50 minutes until golden brown. Slice and serve fresh.

Nutrition: Calories 282 / Total Fat 25.1 g / Saturated Fat 8.8 g / Cholesterol 100 mg
Sodium 117 mg / Total Carbs 9.4 g / Sugar 0.7 g / Fiber 3.2 g / Protein 8 g

85. BREAD WITH WALNUTS AND GARLIC

Preparation Time: 4 hours - Cooking Time: 0 - Servings: 10

Ingredients: 3 cups almond flour - 2 teaspoons dry yeast - 1 cup walnuts - 10 garlic cloves, chopped - 10 tablespoons Olive oil - 1 cup garlic butter, melted - 2 cups water - 2 teaspoons sugar - 2 egg yolks - Sea salt to taste

Directions: Preheat the oven to 290 Degree -320 Degree Fahrenheit and roast the walnuts in the oven for 10-15 minutes until lightly browned and crispy. Set aside to cool completely. Grind the walnuts using a food processor. Melt the unsalted butter by making it softer, by taking it out of the fridge and leaving for around 30 minutes or melt the butter using a frying pan. Meanwhile chop the garlic cloves. Put the almond flour into the bowl and then add in the yeast, sugar, garlic, egg yolks, Olive oil and sea salt and mix until there is a smooth consistency and homogenous mass. Add in the walnuts. Spoon the mixture into the bread machine and add in the water and melted softened garlic butter, mix well. Lubricate the surface of the dough with the water or the egg yolk. Now close the lid and turn the bread machine on the basic/white bread program. After the breakfast wheat bread with garlic is ready, take it out and leave for 1 hour covered with the towel and then you can consume the þread, although we recommend eating your bread after 24 hours.

Nutrition: Calories: 100 / Fat: 4 g / Carbohydrates 4.6 g / Sugar 0 g / Proteins: 2 g

86. PUMPKIN AND SUNFLOWER SEED BREAD

Preparation time: 40 mins - Cooking time: 40 mins - Servings: 10

Ingredients: 1/2 cup ground psyllium husk - 1/2 cup chia seeds - 1/2 cup pumpkin seeds
1/2 cup sunflower seeds - 2 tbsp. ground flaxseed - 1 tsp baking soda - 1/4 tsp salt
3 tbsp. coconut oil, melted - 1 1/4 cup egg whites - 1/2 cup almond milk

Directions: Place all wet ingredients into bread machine pan first.   Add dry ingredients. Set bread machine to the gluten free setting. When the bread is done, remove bread machine pan from the bread machine. Let cool slightly before transferring to a cooling rack. You can store your bread for up to 5 days in the refrigerator.

Nutrition: Calories: 155 / Carbohydrates: 14 g / Protein: 5 g / Fat: 8 g / Fiber 1.3 g

87. SAVORY HERB BLEND BREAD

Preparation time: 40 mins - Cooking time: 40 mins - Servings: 16

Ingredients: 1 cup almond flour - 1/2 cup coconut flour - 1 cup parmesan cheese
3/4 tsp baking powder - 3 eggs - 3 tbsp. coconut oil - 1/2 tbsp. rosemary - 1/2 tsp thyme, ground
1/2 tsp sage, ground - 1/2 tsp oregano - 1/2 tsp garlic powder - 1/2 tsp onion powder -1/4 tsp salt

Directions: Light beat eggs and coconut oil together before adding to bread machine pan. Add all the remaining ingredients to bread machine pan. Set bread machine to the gluten free setting. When the bread is done, remove bread machine pan from the bread machine. Let cool slightly before transferring to a cooling rack. You can store your bread for up to 7 days.

Nutrition: Calories: 170 / Carbohydrates: 6 g / Protein: 9 g / Fat: 15 g / Fiber 1.3 g

88. GARLIC FOCACCIA BREAD

Preparation time: 10 minutes - Cooking time: 20 minutes - Servings: 4

Ingredients: Dry Ingredients : 1 cup almond flour - ¼ cup coconut flour - ½ tsp. xanthan gum
1 tsp. garlic powder - 1 tsp. flaky salt - ½ tsp. baking soda - ½ tsp. baking powder
Wet Ingredients : 2 eggs - 1 tbsp. lemon juice - 2 tsp. olive oil + 2 tbsp. olive oil to drizzle

Directions: Start by preheating the oven to 350 degrees F. Layer a baking sheet with parchment paper. Now, whisk all the dry ingredients in a bowl. Beat lemon juice, oil, and egg in a bowl until well incorporated. Whisk in dry ingredients and mix well until it forms a dough.   Spread the dough on a baking sheet and cover it with aluminum foil. Bake for 10 minutes approximately then remove the foil. Drizzle olive oil on top and bake for another 10 minutes uncovered. Garnish with basil and Italian seasoning. Serve.

Nutrition: Calories 301 / Total Fat 26.3 g / Saturated Fat 14.8 g / Cholesterol 322 mg
Sodium 597 mg / Total Carbs 2.6 g / Fiber 0.6 g / Sugar 1.9 g / Protein 12 g

89. KETO ONION BREAD

Preparation Time: 25 minutes - Cooking Time: 2 hours - Servings: 12

Ingredients: 1 ½ cups water / 2 tbsp. + 2 tsp butter, unsalted / 1 ½ tsp. salt
1 tbsp. + 1 tsp. sugar / 2 tbsp. + 2 tsp. non-fat dry milk / 4 cups almond flour
2 tsp. active dry yeast / 4 tbsps. dry onion soup mix

Directions: Add all ingredients except dry onion mix in the bread machine pan according to the list above. Close the lid cover. Select BASIC cycle on your bread machine and then press START. Your machine will ping after around 30 to 40 minutes. This is your signal to add whatever fruit, nut or flavoring you wish to add to your dough. Pause your bread machine and add the dry onion soup mix. Press START again and allow the cycle to continue. Once your loaf is finish, transfer it to a cooling rack. Slice and serve with cream cheese or butter or as a soup side dish.

Nutrition: Calories: 328 / Total Fat: 15.9 g / Cholesterol: 39 mg / Sodium: 772 mg
Total Carbohydrate: 40.8 g / Protein: 6.4 g

90. KETO SUNDRIED TOMATO QUICK BREAD

Preparation Time: 10 minutes - Cooking Time: 2 hours - Servings: 10

Ingredients: 2 ¼ cup almond flour - 1 tbsp. baking powder - 1 tsp. kosher salt - 3 large eggs
1 ½ cup buttermilk - 6 tbsp. canola oil - 1 tbsp. dried basil - 1 cup sundried tomato roughly chopped

Directions: Place all the fixings in your bread machine bucket except for basil and sundried tomato. Secure the lid cover. Select the QUICK BREAD setting on your bread machine then press START. Wait for the ping or the fruit and nut signal to open the lid and add the basil and sundried tomato. Place a cover and press START to continue. When the cycle finishes, transfer the loaf to a wire rack and let it cool. Slice and serve.

Nutrition: Calories: 182 / Total Fat: 5.1 g / Cholesterol: 0 mg / Sodium: 318 mg
Total Carbohydrate: 31.3 g / Protein: 2.7 g

91. FLAX SEED BREAD

Preparation time: 10 minutes - Cooking time: 20 minutes - Servings: 6

Ingredients: 2 cups flax seed, ground - 1 tablespoon baking powder - 1 and ½ cups protein isolate - A pinch of salt - 6 egg whites, whisked - 1 egg, whisked - ¾ cup water - 3 tablespoons coconut oil, melted - ¼ cup stevia

Directions: In a bowl, mix all dry ingredients and stir well. In a separate bowl, mix the egg whites and the rest of the wet ingredients, stir well and combine the 2 mixtures. Stir the bread and mix well. Pour into a loaf pan and bake at 350 degrees F for 20 minutes. Cool the bread down, slice and serve.

Nutrition: Calories 263 / Fat 17 g / Fiber 4 g / Carbs 2 g / Protein 20 g

92. ALMOND BREAD WITH HAZELNUTS AND GARLIC

Preparation time: 25 minutes - Cooking time: 0 - Servings: 8

Ingredients: 10 garlic cloves, chopped - 1 cup of hazelnuts - 3 cups of almond flour
2 teaspoons dry yeast - 1 cup of garlic butter, melted - 2 teaspoons sugar - 10 tablesp. Olive oil
2 cups of water -2 egg yolks - Sea salt to taste

Directions: Preheat the oven to 300 degree – 320-degree F and roast the hazelnuts in the oven for 10-15 minutes until lightly browned and crispy. Keep aside to cool wholly. Blend the hazelnuts using a food processor. Melt the butter using a frying pan. Chop the garlic cloves. Put the almond flour into the bowl and then add in the yeast, sugar, garlic, egg yolks, Olive oil, and sea salt and mix until there is a smooth consistency. Add in the hazelnuts. Spoon the mixture into the bread machine and add in the water and melted softened garlic butter, mix well.   Lubricate the surface of the dough with the water or the egg yolk. Now close the lid and turn the bread machine on the basic/white bread program. Allow to cool or place in refrigerator and then enjoy it.

Nutrition: Calories: 113 / Fat: 2 g / Carbohydrates 3.9 g / Proteins: 5 g

93. KETO ZUCCHINI BREAD

Preparation Time: 15 minutes - Cooking Time: 58 min - Servings: 12

Ingredients: 3 ounces almond flour - 2 ounces coconut flour - 1/2 teaspoon salt
1/2 teaspoon pepper - 2 teaspoons heating powder - 1 teaspoon thickener - 5 enormous eggs
2/3 cup margarine dissolved - 4 ounces cheddar ground - 6 ounces zucchini ground and fluid crushed out - 6 ounces bacon diced

Directions: Preheat broiler to 175C/350F. In an enormous bowl include the almond flour, coconut flour, salt, pepper, preparing powder and thickener. Blend well. Include the eggs and softened spread and blend well. Overlap through ¾ of the cheddar, alongside the zucchini and bacon. Spoon into your lubed 9in clay portion dish (if utilizing a meat dish, line with material paper) and prepare for 35 minutes, expel from the stove and top with the rest of the cheddar. Prepare for another 10-15 minutes, until the cheddar has caramelized and a stick confesses all. Leave to cool for 20 minutes. Cut into 12 cuts and appreciate warm.

Nutrition: Calories 270 / Fat 15 g / Fiber 3 g / Carbs 5 g / Protein 9 g

94. KETO SPINACH BREAD

Preparation time: 10 minutes - Cooking time: 30 minutes - Servings: 10

Ingredients: ½ cup spinach, chopped - 1 tablespoon olive oil - 1 cup water - 3 cups almond flour - A pinch of salt and black pepper - 1 tablespoon stevia - 1 teaspoon baking powder
1 teaspoon baking soda - ½ cup cheddar, shredded

Directions: In a bowl, mix the flour, with salt, pepper, stevia, baking powder, baking soda and the cheddar and stir well. Add the remaining ingredients, stir the batter really well and pour it into a lined loaf pan. Cook at 350 degrees F for 30 minutes, cool the bread down, slice and serve.

Nutrition: Calories 142 / Fat 7 g / Fiber 3 g /Carbs 5 g / Protein 6 g

95. HERBED GARLIC BREAD

Preparation time: 10 minutes - Cooking time: 45 minutes - Servings: 10

Ingredients: ½ cup coconut flour - 8 tbsp. melted butter, cooled - 1 tsp. baking powder
6 large eggs - 1 tsp. garlic powder - 1 tsp. rosemary, dried - ¼ tsp. salt - ½ tsp. onion powder

Directions: Prepare bread machine loaf pan greasing it with cooking spray. In a bowl, add coconut flour, baking powder, onion, garlic, rosemary, and salt into a bowl. Combine and mix well. Into another bowl, add eggs and beat until bubbly on top. Add melted butter into the bowl with the eggs and beat until mixed. Following the instructions on your machine's manual, mix the dry ingredients into the wet ingredients and pour in the bread machine loaf pan, taking care to follow how to mix in the baking powder. Place the bread pan in the machine, and select the basic bread setting, together with the bread size and crust type, if available, then press start once you have closed the lid of the machine. When the bread is ready, using oven mitts, remove the bread pan from the machine. Let it cool before slicing. Cool, slice, and enjoy.

Nutrition: Calories 147 / Fat 12.5 g / Carb 3.5 g / Protein 4.6 g

96. CINNAMON ASPARAGUS BREAD

Preparation time: 10 minutes - Cooking time: 45 minutes - Servings: 8

Ingredients: 1 cup stevia - ¾ cup coconut oil, melted - 1 and ½ cups almond flour
2 eggs, whisked - A pinch of salt - 1 teaspoon baking soda - 1 teaspoon cinnamon powder
2 cups asparagus, chopped - Cooking spray

Directions: In a bowl, mix all the ingredients except the cooking spray and stir the batter really well. Pour this batter into a loaf pan greased with cooking spray and bake at 350 degrees F for 45 minutes, cool the bread down, slice and serve.

Nutrition: Calories 165 / Fat 6 g / Fiber 3 g / Carbs 5 g / Protein 6 g

97. KALE AND CHEESE BREAD

Preparation time: 10 minutes - Cooking time: 1 hour - Servings: 8

Ingredients: 2 cups kale, chopped - 1 cup warm water - 1 teaspoon baking powder
1 teaspoon baking soda - 2 tablespoons olive oil - 2 teaspoons stevia - 1 cup parmesan, grated
3 cups almond flour - A pinch of salt - 1 egg - 2 tablespoons basil, chopped

Directions: In a bowl, mix the flour, salt, parmesan, stevia, baking soda and baking powder and stir. Add the rest of the ingredients gradually and stir the dough well. Transfer it to a lined loaf pan, cook at 350 degrees F for 1 hour, cool down, slice and serve.

Nutrition: Calories 231 / Fat 7 g / Fiber 2 g / Carbs 5 g / Protein 7 g

98. RED BELL PEPPER BREAD

Preparation time: 10 minutes - Cooking time: 30 minutes - Servings: 12

Ingredients: 1 and ½ cups red bell peppers, chopped - 1 teaspoon baking powder
1 teaspoon baking soda - 2 tablespoons warm water - 1 and ¼ cups parmesan, grated
A pinch of salt - 4 cups almond flour - 2 tablespoons ghee, melted - 1/3 cup almond milk - 1 egg

Directions: In a bowl, mix the flour with salt, parmesan, baking powder, baking soda and the bell peppers and stir well. Add the rest of the ingredients and stir the bread batter well. Transfer it to a lined loaf pan and bake at 350 degrees F for 30 minutes. Cool the bread down, slice and serve.

Nutrition: Calories 100 / Fat 5 g / Fiber 1 g / Carbs 4 g / Protein 4 g

99. SWEET POTATO BREAD

Preparation time: 1 hour 25 minutes - Cooking time: 12-14 minutes - Servings: 10

Ingredients: 1 cup of cooked and mashed sweet potatoes - Extract from vanilla, three teaspoons - Cloves ground, 0.5 tsp. - Cinnamon, 0.5 teaspoon - Nutmeg, ground, 0.5 tsp. Baking powder, 0.5 tsp. - Baking soda, a quarter teaspoon - Salt, 0.5 teaspoon - Eggs, five
½ cup of pure maple syrup - tsp. of coconut oil that is melted - ¾ cup of coconut flour
1 ½ tsp. of active dry yeast

Directions: Get a mixing container and combine the coconut flour, cloves ground, nutmeg ground, cinnamon, baking powder, salt, and baking soda. Get another mixing container and combine the pure vanilla extract, eggs, pure maple syrup, mashed fresh sweet potatoes, and melted coconut oil. As per the instructions on the manual of your machine, pour the ingredients in the bread pan, also following the instructions for the yeast. Place the bread pan in the machine, and select the basic bread setting, together with the bread size and crust type, if available, then press start once you have closed the lid of the machine. When the bread is ready, extract it, and place it on a metallic mesh surface to cool completely before cutting and eating it.

Nutrition: Calories 91 / Fat 1.59 g / Fiber 1.3 g / Carbs 17.72 g / Protein 1.74 g

100. BEET BREAD

Preparation time: 35 minutes - Cooking Time: 35 Minutes - Servings: 6

Ingredients: 1 cup warm water - 3 ½ cups almond flour - 1 and ½ cups beet puree
2 tablespoons olive oil - A pinch of salt - 1 teaspoon stevia - 1 teaspoon baking powder
1 teaspoon baking soda

Directions: Add all ingredients gradually in the bread machine's pan, following the manufacturer's instructions for mixing dry and wet ingredients. Set the bread machine to the basic bread setting. When the bread is done, remove bread machine pan from the bread machine. Let cool slightly before transferring to a cooling rack. Cool the bread down, slice and serve.

Nutrition: Calories 200 / Fat 8 g / Fiber 3 g / Carbs 5 g / Protein 6 g

101. BEETROOT BREAD

Preparation time: 30 minutes - Cooking time: 45 minutes - Servings: 2

Ingredients: 1 cup of grated fresh beetroot - Almond flour, one cup - Coconut flour, half a cup Nutmeg ground, half a teaspoon - Cinnamon ground, a quarter teaspoon - Active dry yeast, two teaspoons - Swerve sweetener, third a cup full - ½ cup of warm water Butter, unsalted & melted four teasp. - Roasted and sliced walnuts, a third cup full - 1 tsp. of baking powder ¼ tsp. of salt

Directions: Get a mixing container and combine the almond flour, the coconut flour, roasted walnuts, Swerve sweetener, cinnamon ground, nutmeg powder, and baking powder. Get another container and combine the warm water, shredded beetroot, and the melted unsalted butter. As per the instructions on the manual of your machine, pour the ingredients in the bread pan, taking care to follow how to mix in the yeast. Place the bread pan in the machine, and select the sweet bread setting, together with the crust type, if available, then press start once you have closed the lid of the machine. When the bread is ready, using oven mitts, remove the bread pan from the machine. Use a stainless spatula to extract the bread from the pan and turn the pan upside down on a metallic rack where the bread will cool off before slicing it.

Nutrition: Calories 854 / Fat 42.59 g / Fiber 5 g / Carbs 102.12 g / Protein 21.93 g

102. TOMATO BREAD

Preparation time: 15 minutes - Cooking Time: ¾ Hour - Servings: 1.5 Lb. /16 Slices

Ingredients: 4 whole eggs - 2 Tbsp. salted butter, melted - 1 cup flaxseed meal - 4 tsp. oat fiber 2 tsp. keto baking powder - 1½ tsp. xanthan gum - ¼ tsp sea salt - ½ tsp. dried basil - ¼ tsp. garlic powder - 2 Tbsp. sun-dried tomatoes, diced - ¼ cup parmesan, grated

Directions: Prepare all of the ingredients for your bread and gather your measuring tools (a cup, a spoon, kitchen scales). Carefully whisk eggs and butter together. Pour all the ingredients into the bread machine pan. Close the cover. Set your bread machine program to CAKE for 30 – 45 minutes (depending on the bread machine model) and choose the crust color LIGHT. Press START. Help the bread machine knead the dough with a spatula, if necessary. Before the baking mode begins, sprinkle the top with grated parmesan. After baking for 20 minutes, check for doneness with a toothpick. Wait until the program is complete. When done, take the bucket out and let it cool for 5-10 minutes. Shake the loaf from the pan and let cool for 30 minutes on a cooling rack. Slice, serve with a soup or a salad, and enjoy the taste of fragrant homemade keto bread.

Nutrition: Calories 88 /Net Carbs 0.6 g /Total Fat 6.1 g / Saturated Fat 2.4 g / Cholesterol 48 g Sodium 243 mg / Total Carbohydrate 2.6 g

103. HEARTY CHEESY BROCCOLI BREAD

Preparation time: 35 minutes - Cooking Time: 30 Minutes - Servings: 4

Ingredients: 5 eggs, whisked - 2 teaspoons baking powder - 1 cup cheddar, shredded
1 cup broccoli florets, separated - 4 tablespoons coconut flour - Cooking spray

Directions: In a bowl, mix all the ingredients except the cooking spray and stir the batter really well. Pour batter in the bread machine pan pre-greased with cooking spray. Set the bread machine to the basic bread setting. When the bread is done, remove bread machine pan from the bread machine. Let cool slightly before transferring to a cooling rack. Cool the bread down, slice / serve.

Nutrition: Calories 123 / Fat 6 g / Fiber 1 g / Carbs 3 g / Protein 6 g

104. HOT RED PEPPER BREAD

Preparation time: 15 minutes - Cooking Time: 1 hour - Servings: 12

Ingredients: 2 cups of dried, roasted hot red peppers, crushed - 2 tsp. of active dry yeast
1 tsp. of pepper powder - 2 eggs - 2 tsp. of warm water - ½ cup of unsweetened almond milk
Salt, half a teaspoon - 1 ½ tsp. of baking powder - Almond flour, two cups - Coconut flour, one cup - Melted unsalted butter, two teaspoons

Directions: Get a mixing container and combine the almond flour, dried and crushed roasted hot red peppers, salt, coconut flour, and baking powder. Get another mixing container and combine the eggs, unsweetened almond milk, warm water, and melted unsalted butter. As per the instructions on the manual of your machine, pour the ingredients in the bread pan, following the instructions of adding the yeast. Place the bread pan in the machine, and select the sweet bread setting, together with the bread size and crust type, if available, then press start once you have closed the lid of the machine. When the bread is ready, extract it, and place it on a metallic mesh surface to cool completely before cutting and eating it.

Nutrition: Calories 107 / Fat 5.45 g / Fiber 1.8 g / Carbs 7.86 g / Protein 8.22 g

105. HERBED KETO BREAD

Preparation time: 5 minutes - Cooking Time: 40 Minutes - Servings: 8

Ingredients: 3 cups coconut flour - 1 teaspoon baking powder - 1 teaspoon baking soda
2 teaspoons stevia - 1 ½ cups warm water - ½ teaspoon basil, dried - 1 teaspoon oregano, dried
½ teaspoon thyme, dried - ½ teaspoon marjoram, dried - 2 tablespoons olive oil

Directions: In a bowl, mix the flour with baking powder, baking soda, stevia, basil, oregano, thyme, and the marjoram and stir. Add the rest of the ingredients, stir well and transfer the dough in the bread machine loaf pan pre-greased with cooking spray. However, take a look to the manufacturer's instructions for mixing dry and wet ingredients. Place the bread pan in the machine, and select the basic bread setting, together with the bread size, if available, then press start once you have closed the lid of the machine. When the bread is ready, using oven mitts, remove the bread pan from the machine. Cool the bread down before serving.

Nutrition: Calories 200 / Fat 7 g / Fiber 3 g / Carbs 5 g / Protein 6 g

106. LIGHT CORNBREAD

Preparation time: 15 minutes - Cooking Time: 40 Minutes - Servings: 8

Ingredients: Eggs, four - Almond flour, one and a half cup full - Swerve Keto sweetener half a cup - Extract of vanilla, one teaspoon - Baking powder, one teaspoon - Unsalted melted butter, four teaspoons

Directions: Prepare a mixing container, where you will combine the almond flour, Swerve sweetener, and baking powder. In another mixing container, combine the eggs, pure vanilla extract, and unsalted melted butter. As per the instructions on the manual of your machine, pour the ingredients in the bread pan, taking care to follow how to mix in the yeast. Place the bread pan in the machine, and select the basic bread setting, together with the bread size and crust type, if available, then press start once you have closed the lid of the machine. When the bread is ready, using oven mitts, remove the bread pan from the machine. Use a stainless spatula to extract the bread from the pan, and turn the pan upside down on a metallic rack where the bread will cool off before slicing it.

Nutrition: Calories 66 / Fat 1.78 g / Fiber 0.1 g / Carbs 11 g / Protein 1.16 g

107. ZUCCHINI LEMON BREAD

Preparation time: 5 minutes - Cooking Time: 40 Minutes - Servings: 12

Ingredients: 2 cups of almond flour - Salt, 3/4 teaspoon - Baking powder, one teaspoon Baking soda, half a teaspoon - Zucchini grated; two cups full - Extract of vanilla, two teaspoons Swerve sweetener, a third cup - zest from 2 lemons - 3 eggs - Melted butter, unsalted, three-quarters of a cup full - Juice of a fresh lemon, two teaspoons - Active dry yeast, one and a half teaspoon

Directions: In a mixing container, combine the almond flour, salt, baking powder, and baking soda. Get another mixing bowl and combine the shredded zucchini, pure vanilla extract, lemon zest, lemon juice, eggs, and unsalted melted butter. As per the instructions on the manual of your machine, pour the ingredients in the bread pan, taking care to follow how to mix in the yeast. Place the bread pan in the machine, and select the basic bread setting, together with the bread size and crust type, if available, then press start once you have closed the lid of the machine. When the bread is ready, using oven mitts, remove the bread pan from the machine. Use a stainless spatula to extract the bread from the pan and turn the pan upside down on a metallic rack where the bread will cool off before slicing it.

Nutrition: Calories 230 / Fat 17.98 g / Fiber 0.2 g / Carbs 15.23 g / Protein 2.58 g

108. ONION BREAD

Preparation time: 20 minutes - Cooking time: 5 minutes - Servings: 6

Ingredients: 1 red onion diced and sautéed with ½ tsp. of butter until golden brown - 3 tsp. of melted unsalted butter - Salt, a quarter teaspoon - Ground garlic, a quarter teaspoon - psyllium husk flour, three teaspoons - 5 eggs - Baking powder, half a teaspoon - Active dry yeast, three-quarters of a teaspoon - Onion powder, half a teaspoon - Almond flour, one cup

Directions: Get a mixing container and combine the almond flour, salt, psyllium husk flour, ground onion, baking powder, and ground garlic. Get another mixing container and mix the melted unsalted butter, eggs, and sautéed onions. As per the instructions on the manual of your machine, pour the ingredients in the bread pan, also following the instructions for the yeast. Place the bread pan in the machine, and select the basic bread setting, together with the bread size and crust type, if available, then press start once you have closed the lid of the machine. When the bread is ready, extract it, and place it on a metallic mesh surface to cool completely before cutting and eating it.

Nutrition: Calories 127 / Fat 9.48 g / Fiber 0.3 g / Carbs 2.07 g / Protein 7.97 g

SWEET BREAD

109. RASPBERRY BREAD

Preparation time: 10 minutes - Cooking Time: 50 minutes - Servings: 12 slices

Ingredients: 1 cup (100g) raspberries - ¼ cup (50g) of your favorite sugar substitute 1½ tsp. keto baking powder - 2 cups (200g) almond flour - 4 Tbsp. sour cream - 4 Tbsp. unsalted butter, melted - 2 whole eggs - 1 tsp. vanilla - 1 tsp. lemon extract - ½ lemon, juiced

Directions : Prepare all of the ingredients for your bread and gather your measuring tools (a cup, a spoon, kitchen scales). Add all of the ingredients (except the raspberries) to the bread machine pan following the instructions for your device. Close the cover. Set your bread machine program to CAKE for 40 – 50 minutes. After the signal, add the raspberries to the dough. Press START. Check for doneness with a toothpick. The approximate baking time is 45 minutes. Wait until the program is complete. When done, take the bucket out and let it cool for 5-10 minutes. Shake the loaf from the pan and let cool for 30 minutes on a cooling rack. Slice, serve, and enjoy the taste of fragrant sweet keto bread.

Nutrition: Calories 168 / Net Carbs 8.3 g / Total Fat 14.8 g / Saturated Fat 3.8 g
Cholesterol 39 g / Sodium 138 mg / Total Carbohydrate 11.1 g

110. BLUEBERRY BREAD

Preparation time: 10 minutes - Cooking Time: 50 minutes - Servings: 12 slices

Ingredients: ½ cup (50g) blueberries - 1/3 cup (67g) of your favorite sugar substitute 2 tsp. keto baking powder - 2 cups (200g) almond flour - 4 Tbsp. sour cream - 4 Tbsp. unsalted butter, melted - 2 whole eggs - 1 tsp. vanilla

Directions : Prepare all of the ingredients for your bread and gather your measuring tools (a cup, a spoon, kitchen scales). In a large bowl, beat eggs with an electric mixer well. Pour them into the bread machine pan. Add all other ingredients. Close the cover. Set your bread machine program to CAKE for 45 – 60 minutes (depends on your device). Press START. After the signal indicating the beginning of the BAKE mode, add the blueberries. After 35 minutes of baking, start checking for doneness using a toothpick. The approximate baking time is 45 - 50 minutes. Wait until the program is complete. When done, take the bucket out and let it cool for 5-10 minutes. Shake the loaf from the pan and let it cool for 30 minutes on a cooling rack. Slice, serve, and enjoy the taste of fragrant sweet keto bread.

Nutrition: Calories 165 / Net Carbs 9.8 g / Total Fat 14.8 g / Saturated Fat 3.8 g
Cholesterol 39 g / Sodium 169 mg / Total Carbohydrate 12 g

111. CHOCOLATE BREAD

Preparation time: 10 minutes - Cooking Time: 60 – 70 minutes - Servings: 12 slices

Ingredients: 6 whole eggs, well-beaten - ½ tsp. vanilla - ½ tsp. Stevia - 2 tsp. apple cider vinegar - 4 oz. (1 stick/113g) salted butter, melted - 1 oz. (28g) unsweetened baking chocolate, melted - ¾ cups coconut flour - ½ cup your favorite keto sweetener - ¼ cup (25g) unsweetened cocoa powder - 1 tsp. keto baking powder - ½ tsp. baking soda - ½ tsp. instant keto coffee ½ tsp. sea salt - ¼ tsp. xanthan gum - 2 Tbsp. sugar-free chocolate chips (for garnish)

Directions: Prepare all of the ingredients for your bread and gather your measuring tools (a cup, a spoon, kitchen scales). In a large bowl, mix all of the dry ingredients. In a small bowl, beat the eggs with an electric mixer. Pour eggs and all of the wet ingredients into the bread machine pan. Cover them with the dry ingredients. Close the cover. Set your bread machine program to CAKE for 60 minutes. The time may vary depending on your device. Press START. Help the machine to knead the dough, if necessary. After 40 minutes of baking, start checking for doneness using a toothpick. The approximate baking time is 45 - 55 minutes. Wait until the program is complete. When done, take the bucket out and let it cool for 5-10 minutes. Shake the loaf from the pan and let it cool for 30 minutes on a cooling rack. Slice, serve, and enjoy the taste of fragrant chocolate keto bread.

Nutrition: Calories 129 / Net Carbs 12.1 g / Total Fat 12 g / Saturated Fat 6.9 g
Cholesterol 103 g / Sodium 285 mg / Total Carbohydrate 13.5 g

112. BANANA BREAD

Preparation time: 10 minutes - Cooking Time: 60 – 70 minutes - Servings: 16 slices

Ingredients: 2½ cup (300g) almond flour - 1 cup (240g) mashed banana (2 large bananas) 6 large organic eggs, beaten - 4 Tbsp. ghee, melted - ½ cup erythritol - 2 Tbsp. cinnamon 1 Tbsp. keto baking powder - ½ cup (60g) walnuts, crushed - ¼ tsp. ground nutmeg

Directions: Prepare all of the ingredients for your bread and gather your measuring tools (a cup, a spoon, kitchen scales). In a large bowl, mix all of the dry ingredients. In a small bowl, beat the eggs with an electric mixer. Pour eggs and all of the wet ingredients into the bread machine pan. Cover them with the dry ingredients. Close the cover. Set your bread machine program to DOUGH. The time may vary depending on your device. Press START. Help the machine to knead the dough, if necessary. After the program completes, start the Bake mode for 55 minutes. After 45 minutes of baking, start checking for doneness using a toothpick. The approximate baking time is 45 - 60 minutes. Wait until the program is complete. When done, take the bucket out and let it cool for 5-10 minutes. Shake the loaf from the pan and let it cool for 30 minutes on a cooling rack. Slice, serve, and enjoy the taste of fragrant banana keto bread.

Nutrition: Calories 191 / Net Carbs 11.9 g / Total Fat 16.2 g / Saturated Fat 3.3 g
Cholesterol 78 g / Sodium 173 mg / Total Carbohydrate 14.8 g

113. AVOCADO BREAD

Preparation time: 10 minutes - Cooking Time: 60 – 70 minutes - Servings: 14 slices

Ingredients: 4 avocados, mashed - 2 cups almond flour - 1 cup coconut flour
½ cup monk fruit sweetener - 5 Tbsp. avocado oil - 4 Tbsp. unsweetened cocoa powder
½ tsp. kosher salt - 1 tsp. baking soda - 1 tsp. vanilla extract - 1 cup chocolate chips

Directions: Prepare all of the ingredients for your bread and gather your measuring tools (a cup, a spoon, kitchen scales). In a large bowl, mix all of the dry ingredients. In a blender, combine all of the wet ingredients. Pour all of the wet ingredients into the bread machine pan. Cover them with the dry ingredients. Add half of the chocolate chips. Close the cover. Set your bread machine program to CAKE. The time may vary depending on your device. Press START. Help the machine to knead the dough, if necessary. Before the baking, top the bread with the remaining ½ cup of chocolate chips. After 45 minutes of baking, start checking for doneness using a toothpick. The approximate baking time is 45 - 60 minutes. Wait until the program is complete. When done, take the bucket out and let it cool for 5-10 minutes. Shake the loaf from the pan and let it cool for 30 minutes on a cooling rack. Slice, serve, and enjoy the taste of fragrant chocolate avocado keto bread.

Nutrition: Calories 290 / Net Carbs 10.7 g / Total Fat 24.1 g / Saturated Fat 5.8 g
Cholesterol 3 g / Sodium 187 mg / Total Carbohydrate 17.5 g

114. GINGERBREAD CAKE

Preparation time: 10 minutes - Cooking Time: 45 minutes - Servings: 10 slices

Ingredients: 4 large organic eggs - ¼ cup (60ml, 4oz) unsalted organic butter, melted
1 tsp. vanilla extract - ¾ cup (150g, 5 1/3 oz.) granulated Swerve - ¾ cup (90g, 3 1/5 oz.)
coconut flour - 1 tsp. keto baking powder - 2 tsp. ground ginger - 2 tsp. ground cinnamon
½ tsp. ground allspice - ½ tsp. ground nutmeg - ½ tsp. ground clove - ¼ tsp. kosher salt
For Icing: ½ cup (120g, 1.2oz) cream cheese, softened - ¼ cup (40g, 1.4oz) Swerve, powdered
1 tsp. vanilla extract - ¼ cup (30g) walnuts, chopped

Directions : Prepare all of the ingredients for your bread and gather your measuring tools (a cup, a spoon, kitchen scales). Whisk together the eggs, vanilla, and the unsalted butter. In a large bowl, mix all of the dry ingredients. Pour all of the wet ingredients into the bread machine pan. Cover them with the dry ingredients. Close the cover. Set your bread machine program to CAKE. The time may vary depending on your device. Press START. Help the machine to knead the dough, if necessary. After 30 minutes of baking, start checking for doneness using a toothpick. The approximate baking time is 40 - 45 minutes. Wait until the program is complete. When done, take the bucket out and let it cool for 5-10 minutes. Shake the loaf from the pan and let it cool for 30 minutes on a cooling rack. Slice, serve, and enjoy the taste of fragrant gingerbread cake.

Nutrition: Calories 140 / Net Carbs 13.3 g / Total Fat 12.9 g / Saturated Fat 6.5 g
Cholesterol 99 g / Sodium 201 mg / Total Carbohydrate 14.3 g

115. LEMON BREAD

Preparation time: 10 minutes - Cooking Time: 1 hour - Servings: 12 slices

Ingredients: 9.5 oz. (270g) almond flour - ½ tsp. keto baking powder - ½ cup erythritol 2 Tbsp. poppy seeds - Zest of 2 lemons - 2 Tbsp. lemon juice - 3 Tbsp. unsalted butter, melted 6 whole eggs - For Icing: ½ cup powdered erythritol - 1 Tbsp. lemon juice - 2 Tbsp. water

Directions: Prepare all of the ingredients for your bread and gather your measuring tools (a cup, a spoon, kitchen scales). Put all ingredients into the bread machine pan. Close the cover. Set your bread machine program to CAKE. The time may vary depending on your device. Press START. Help the machine to knead the dough, if necessary. After 40 minutes of baking, start checking for doneness using a toothpick. The approximate baking time is 45 - 55 minutes. Wait until the program is complete. When done, take the bucket out and let it cool for 5 - 10 minutes. Shake the loaf from the pan and let it cool for 30 minutes on a cooling rack. Make the icing in a small bowl, mixing all the ingredients together. Drizzle it over the bread. Slice, serve, and enjoy the taste of fragrant lemon bread.

Nutrition: Calories 193 / Net Carbs 12.9 g / Total Fat 17 g / Saturated Fat 3.4 g Cholesterol 89 g / Sodium 85 mg / Total Carbohydrate 15.6 g

116. HOLIDAY BREAD

Preparation time: 30 min - Cooking Time: 1 hour - Servings: 2 pounds / 12 slices

Ingredients: 2½ cups (250g) almond flour - 2 cups (140 g) whey isolate - 1 cup (240 ml) lukewarm water - ¼ cup (60 ml) almond milk - ½ cup (100 g) powdered erythritol - ½ cup (100 g) butter, melted - 1½ Tbsp. keto baking powder - 2 tsp. xanthan gum - ½ tsp. sea salt For Icing: ½ cup powdered erythritol - 1 Tbsp. lemon juice - 2 Tbsp. water

Directions: Prepare all of the ingredients for your bread and gather your measuring tools (a cup, a spoon, kitchen scales). Put all ingredients into the bread machine pan. Close the cover. Set your bread machine program to CAKE. The time may vary depending on your device. Press START. Help the machine to knead the dough, if necessary. After 25 minutes of baking, start checking for doneness using a toothpick. The approximate baking time is 30 - 35 minutes. Wait until the program is complete. When done, take the bucket out and let it cool for 5 - 10 minutes. Shake the loaf from the pan and let it cool for 30 minutes on a cooling rack. Make the icing in a small bowl, mixing all the ingredients together. Drizzle it over the bread. Slice, serve, and enjoy the taste of fragrant sweet bread.

Nutrition: Calories 130 / Net Carbs 5 g / Total Fat 11.8 g / Saturated Fat 6.1 g Cholesterol 21 g / Sodium 248 mg / Total Carbohydrate 12 g

117. CINNAMON BREAD

Preparation time: 10 min - Cooking time: 4 hours - Servings: 2 pounds / 10 slices

Ingredients: 3 tablespoons sour cream - 3 eggs, pasteurized - 2 teaspoons vanilla extract, unsweetened - ¼ cup / 60 grams melted butter, grass-fed, unsalted - 2 cups / 200 grams almond flour - 1/3 cup / 65 grams erythritol sweetener - 2 tablespoons cinnamon - 1 teaspoon baking soda - 1 teaspoon baking powder

Directions: Gather all the ingredients for the bread and plug in the bread machine having the capacity of 2 pounds of bread recipe. Take a large bowl, place sour cream in it and then beat in eggs, vanilla, and butter until combined. Take a separate large bowl, place flour in it, and then stir in sweetener, cinnamon, baking powder, and soda until mixed. Add egg mixture into the bread bucket, top with flour mixture, shut the lid, select the "basic/white" cycle setting and then press the up/down arrow button to adjust baking time according to your bread machine; it will take 3 to 4 hours. Then press the crust button to select light crust if available, and press the "start/stop" button to switch on the bread machine. When the bread machine beeps, open the lid, then take out the bread basket and lift out the bread. Let bread cool on a wire rack for 1 hour, then cut it into ten slices and serve.

Nutrition: Cal 169 / Fat 5.4 g / Protein 4.2 g / Carb 2 g / Fiber 2.2 g / Net Carb 14,5 g

118. LEMON RASPBERRY LOAF

Preparation time: 10 min - Cooking time: 4 hours - Servings: 2 pounds / 12 slices

Ingredients: 2 eggs, pasteurized - 4 tablespoons sour cream - 1 teaspoon vanilla extract, unsweetened - 1 teaspoon lemon extract, unsweetened - 4 tablespoons butter, grass-fed, unsalted, melted - 1/4 cup / 50 grams erythritol sweetener - 2 tablespoons lemon juice ½ cup / 100 grams raspberries preserves - 2 cups / 200 grams almond flour - 1 ½ teaspoons baking powder

Directions: Gather all the ingredients for the bread and plug in the bread machine having the capacity of 2 pounds of bread recipe. Take a large bowl, place flour in it, and then stir in baking soda until mixed. Take a separate large bowl, crack eggs in it, beat in sour cream, extracts, butter, sweetener, and lemon juice until blended and then stir in raspberry preserve until just combined. Add egg mixture into the bread bucket, top with flour mixture, shut the lid, select the "basic/white" cycle setting and then press the up/down arrow button to adjust baking time according to your bread machine; it will take 3 to 4 hours. Then press the crust button to select light crust if available, and press the "start/stop" button to switch on the bread machine. When the bread machine beeps, open the lid, then take out the bread basket and lift out the bread. Let bread cool on a wire rack for 1 hour, then cut it into twelve slices and serve.

Nutrition: 171 Cal / 14.3 g Fat / 4.6 g Protein / 5 g Carb / 2.4 g Fiber / 2.6 g Net Carb

119. WALNUT BREAD

Preparation time: 10 min - Cooking time: 4 hours - Servings: 1 ½ pounds / 10 slices

Ingredients: 4 eggs, pasteurized - 2 tablespoons apple cider vinegar - 4 tablespoons coconut oil - 1/2 cup / 120 ml lukewarm water - 1 cup / 200 grams walnuts chopped - ½ cup / 65 grams coconut flour - 1 tablesp. baking powder - 2 tablesp. psyllium husk powder - 1/2 teaspoon salt

Directions: Gather all the ingredients for the bread and plug in the bread machine having the capacity of 2 pounds of bread recipe. Take a large bowl, crack eggs in it, beat in vinegar, oil, and water until blended and stir in walnuts until just mixed. Take a separate large bowl, place flour in it, and then stir in baking powder, husk powder, and salt until mixed. Add egg mixture into the bread bucket, top with flour mixture, shut the lid, select the "basic/white" cycle setting and then press the up/down arrow button to adjust baking time according to your bread machine; it will take 3 to 4 hours. Then press the crust button to select light crust if available, and press the "start/stop" button to switch on the bread machine. When the bread machine beeps, open the lid, then take out the bread basket and lift out the bread. Let bread cool on a wire rack for 1 hour, then cut it into ten slices and serve.

Nutrition: 201 Cal / 8.1 g Fat / 6 g Protein / 7.5 g Carb / 4.7 g Fiber / 2.8 g Net Carb

120. ALMOND BUTTER BREAD

Preparation time: 10 min - Cooking time: 4 hours - Servings: 1 pound / 12 slices

Ingredients: 3 eggs, pasteurized - 1 cup / 225 grams almond butter - 1 tablespoon apple cider vinegar - 1/2 teaspoon baking soda

Directions: Gather all the ingredients for the bread and plug in the bread machine having the capacity of 1 pound of bread recipe. Crack eggs in a bowl and then beat in butter, vinegar, and baking soda until combined. Add egg mixture into the bread bucket, shut the lid, select the "basic/white" cycle setting and then press the up/down arrow button to adjust baking time according to your bread machine; it will take 3 to 4 hours. Then press the crust button to select light crust if available, and press the "start/stop" button to switch on the bread machine. When the bread machine beeps, open the lid, then take out the bread basket and lift out the bread. Let bread cool on a wire rack for 1 hour, then cut it into twelve slices and serve.

Nutrition: 152 Cal / 13 g Fat / 6.4 g Protein / 5.6 g Carb / 3.1 g Fiber / 2.5 g Net Carb

121. CHOCOLATE ZUCCHINI BREAD

Preparation time: 10 min - Cooking time: 4 hours - Servings: 2 pounds / 14 slices

Ingredients: 1 cup / 200 grams grated zucchini, moisture squeezed thoroughly
1/3 cup / 60 grams ground flaxseed - ½ cup / 100 grams almond flour
1/2 teaspoon salt - 2 ½ teaspoons baking powder - 1 ¼ tablespoon psyllium husk powder
1/3 cup / 60 grams of cocoa powder - 4 eggs, pasteurized - 1 tablespoon coconut cream
5 tablesp. coconut oil - ¾ cup / 150 grams erythritol sweetener - ½ cup / 115 grams sour cream
1 teaspoon vanilla extract, unsweetened - ½ cup / 115 grams sour cream
½ cup / 100 grams chocolate chips, unsweetened

Directions: Wrap zucchini in cheesecloth and twist well until all the moisture is released, set aside until required. Gather all the ingredients for the bread and plug in the bread machine having the capacity of 2 pounds of bread recipe. Take a large bowl, place flaxseed and flour in it, and then stir salt, baking powder, husk, and cocoa powder in it until mixed. Take a separate large bowl, crack eggs in it and then beat in coconut cream, coconut oil, sweetener, and vanilla until combined. Blend in half of the flour mixture, then sour cream and remaining half of flour mixture until incorporated and then fold in chocolate chips until mixed. Add batter into the bread bucket, shut the lid, select the "basic/white" cycle setting and then press the up/down arrow button to adjust baking time according to your bread machine; it will take 3 to 4 hours. Then press the crust button to select light crust if available, and press the "start/stop" button to switch on the bread machine. When the bread machine beeps, open the lid, then take out the bread basket and lift out the bread. Let bread cool on a wire rack for 1 hour, then cut it into fourteen slices and serve.

Nutrition: 187 Cal / 15.9 g Fat / 6.2 g Protein / 8.8 g Carb / 5.2 g Fiber / 3.6 g Net Carb

122. PUMPKIN BREAD

Preparation time: 10 min - Cooking time: 4 hours - Servings: 1 ½ pound / 12 slices

Ingredients: 2 eggs, pasteurized - 1 cup / 225 grams almond butter, unsweetened
2/3 cup / 130 grams erythritol sweetener - 2/3 cup / 150 grams pumpkin puree
1/8 teaspoon ground cloves - 1/2 teaspoon ground cinnamon - 1/8 teaspoon ground ginger
1 teaspoon baking powder - 1/2 teaspoon ground nutmeg

Directions: Gather all the ingredients for the bread and plug in the bread machine having the capacity of 2 pounds of bread recipe. Take a large bowl, crack eggs in it and then beat in remaining ingredients in it in the order described in the ingredients until incorporated. Add batter into the bread bucket, shut the lid, select the "basic/white" cycle setting and then press the up/down arrow button to adjust baking time according to your bread machine; it will take 3 to 4 hours. Then press the crust button to select light crust if available, and press the "start/stop" button to switch on the bread machine. When the bread machine beeps, open the lid, then take out the bread basket and lift out the bread. Let bread cool on a wire rack for 1 hour, then cut it into twelve slices and serve.

Nutrition: 150 Cal / 12.9 g Fat / 6.7 g Protein / 7 g Carb / 2 g Fiber / 5 g Net Carb

123. STRAWBERRY BREAD

Preparation time: 10 min - Cooking time: 4 hours - Servings: 2 pounds / 10 slices

Ingredients: 5 eggs, pasteurized - 1 egg white, pasteurized - 1 1/2 teaspoons vanilla extract, unsweetened - 2 tablespoons heavy whipping cream - 2 tablespoons sour cream
1 cup monk fruit powder - 1 1/2 teaspoons baking powder - 1/2 teaspoon salt
1/2 teaspoon cinnamon - 8 tablespoons butter, melted - ¾ cup / 100 grams coconut flour
¾ cup / 150 grams chopped strawberries

Directions: Gather all the ingredients for the bread and plug in the bread machine having the capacity of 2 pounds of bread recipe. Take a large bowl, crack eggs in it and then beat in egg white, vanilla, heavy cream, sour cream, baking powder, salt, and cinnamon until well combined. Then stir in coconut flour and fold in strawberries until mixed. Add batter into the bread bucket, shut the lid, select the "basic/white" cycle or "low-carb" setting and then press the up/down arrow button to adjust baking time according to your bread machine; it will take 3 to 4 hours. Then press the crust button to select light crust if available, and press the "start/stop" button to switch on the bread machine. When the bread machine beeps, open the lid, then take out the bread basket and lift out the bread. Let bread cool on a wire rack for 1 hour, then cut it into ten slices and serve.

Nutrition: 201 Cal / 16.4 g Fat / 4.7 g Protein / 6.1 g Carb / 3 g Fiber / 3.1 g Net Carb

124. CRANBERRY AND ORANGE BREAD

Preparation time: 10 min - Cooking time: 4 hours - Servings: 1 ½ pound / 12 slices

Ingredients: 1 cup / 200 grams chopped cranberries - 2/3 cup and 3 tablespoons / 175 grams monk fruit powder, divided - 5 eggs, pasteurized - 1 egg white, pasteurized - 2 tablespoons sour cream - 1 1/2 teaspoons orange extract, unsweetened - 1 teaspoon vanilla extract, unsweetened
9 tablespoons butter, grass-fed, unsalted, melted - 9 tablespoons coconut flour - 1 1/2 teaspoons baking powder - 1/4 teaspoon salt

Directions: Take a small bowl, place cranberries in it, and then stir in 4 tablespoons of monk fruit powder until combined, set aside until required. Gather all the ingredients for the bread and plug in the bread machine having the capacity of 2 pounds of bread recipe. Take a large bowl, crack eggs in it, beat in remaining ingredients in it in the order described in the ingredients until incorporated and then fold in cranberries until just mixed. Add batter into the bread bucket, shut the lid, select the "basic/white" cycle or "low-carb" setting and then press the up/down arrow button to adjust baking time according to your bread machine; it will take 3 to 4 hours. Then press the crust button to select light crust if available, and press the "start/stop" button to switch on the bread machine. When the bread machine beeps, open the lid, then take out the bread basket and lift out the bread. Let bread cool on a wire rack for 1 hour, then cut it into twelve slices and serve.

Nutrition: 149 Cal / 13.1 g Fat / 3.9 g Protein / 4 g Carb / 1.5 g Fiber / 2.5 g Net Carb

125. SWEET AVOCADO BREAD

Preparation time: 10 min - Cooking time: 4 hours - Servings: 1 ½ pounds / 12 slices

Ingredients: 3 eggs, pasteurized - 2 tablespoons erythritol sweetener - 1 tablespoon vanilla extract, unsweetened - 1 ½ cups / 300 grams mashed avocado mashed, ripe - 6 tablespoons coconut flour - 3/4 teasp. baking soda - 1/2 teasp. salt - 2 tablesp. cocoa powder, unsweetened

Directions: Gather all the ingredients for the bread and plug in the bread machine having the capacity of 2 pounds of bread recipe. Take a large bowl, crack eggs in it, beat in sweetener and vanilla until fluffy and then mix in avocado. Take a separate large bowl, place flour in it, and then stir in remaining ingredients until mixed. Add egg mixture into the bread bucket, top with flour mixture, shut the lid, select the "basic/white" cycle or "low-carb" setting and then press the up/down arrow button to adjust baking time according to your bread machine; it will take 3 to 4 hours. Then press the crust button to select light crust if available, and press the "start/stop" button to switch on the bread machine. When the bread machine beeps, open the lid, then take out the bread basket and lift out the bread. Let bread cool on a wire rack for 1 hour, then cut it into twelve slices and serve.

Nutrition: 94 Cal / 6.1 g Fat / 4.2 g Protein / 3.2 g Carb / 2.7 g Fiber / 0.5 g Net Carb

126. DELICIOUS CARROT CAKE

Preparation time: 15 minutes - Cooking time: 55 minutes - Servings: 6

Ingredients: 2 large eggs - ½ cup carrots, grated - 1 teaspoon vanilla - 2 tablespoons coconut oil, melted - 3 tablespoons heavy cream - ¼ teaspoon nutmeg - ½ teaspoon cinnamon
1 teaspoon baking powder - 2/3 cup Swerve - 1 cup almond flour
For Frosting: 1 tablespoon heavy cream - ½ teaspoon vanilla - 2 teaspoons fresh lemon juice
3 tablespoons swerve - 4 ounces cream cheese, softened

Directions: Take a cake pan which fits into the instant pot, spray with cooking spray and set aside. Drain excess liquid from grated carrots. In a mixing bowl, mix together almond flour, grated carrots, vanilla, coconut oil, heavy cream, eggs, nutmeg, cinnamon, baking powder, and swerve using a hand mixer until well combined. Pour batter into the prepared cake pan and cover the pan with foil. Add 1 2/3 cup of water to the instant pot, then place steamer rack into the pot. Place cake pan on the steamer rack. Seal the instant pot with the lid and select manual high pressure and set the timer for 45 minutes. Allow releasing pressure naturally for 10 minutes, then release using the Quick release method. Open the lid carefully and remove the cake pan from the pot. Let the cake cool for 30 minutes. Meanwhile, make the frosting. In a large bowl, add heavy cream, vanilla, lemon juice, swerve, and cream cheese and beat using a hand mixer until creamy. Once the cake is cool completely, then frost the cake using prepared cream. Cut cake into slices and serve.

Nutrition: Calories: 289 / Fat: 25.9 g / Carbohydrates: 10.9 g / Protein: 7.9 g

127. PURPLE YAM PANCAKES

Preparation time: 5 minutes - Cooking time: 10 minutes - Servings: 4

Ingredients: ½ cup coconut flour - 4 eggs - 1 cup coconut milk - 1 teaspoon guar gum
½ teaspoon baking powder - 1 tablespoon coconut oil - ¼ cup purple yam puree

Directions: Mix all ingredients in a blender. Preheat a skillet and coat with non-stick spray. Ladle in the batter and cook for 1-2 minutes per side.

Nutrition: Kcal per serve: 347 / Fat: 31 g (76%) / Protein: 11 g (13%) / Carb: 9 g (11%)

128. ALMOND COCONUT CAKE

Preparation time: 10 minutes - Cooking time: 50 minutes - Servings: 8

Ingredients: 2 eggs, lightly beaten - ½ cup heavy cream - ¼ cup coconut oil, melted
1 teaspoon cinnamon - 1 teaspoon baking powder - 1/3 cup Swerve - ½ cup unsweetened
shredded coconut - 1 cup almond flour

Directions: Spray a 6- inch cake pan with cooking spray and set aside. In a large bowl, mix together the almond flour, cinnamon, baking powder, swerve, and shredded coconut. Add eggs, heavy cream, and coconut oil into the almond flour mixture and mix until well combined. Pour batter into the prepared cake pan and cover the pan with foil. Add 2 cups of water into the instant pot, then place a steamer rack in the pot. Place cake pan on top of steamer rack. Seal the instant pot with the lid and select manual high pressure and set the timer for 40 minutes. Once the timer goes off, allow to release pressure naturally for 10 minutes and then release using Quick-release method. Open the lid carefully. Remove the cake pan from the pot and let it cool for 20 minutes. Cut cake into slices and serve.

Nutrition: Calories: 228 / Fat 21.7 g / Carbohydrates: 5.2 g / Protein: 5 g

129. TASTY CHOCOLATE CAKE

Preparation time: 10 minutes - Cooking time: 30 minutes - Servings: 6

Ingredients: 3 large eggs - ¼ cup butter, melted - 1/3 cup heavy cream - 1 teaspoon baking powder - ¼ cup walnuts, chopped - ¼ cup unsweetened cocoa powder - 2/3 cup Swerve
1 cup almond flour

Directions: Spray cake pan with cooking spray and set aside. Add all ingredients into a large mixing bowl and mix using a hand mixer until the mixture looks fluffy. Pour batter into the prepared cake pan. Pour 2 cups of water into the instant pot, then place a steamer rack in the pot. Place cake pan on top of steamer rack. Seal the instant pot with the lid and cook on manual high pressure for 20 minutes. Allow releasing pressure naturally for 10 minutes, then release using the Quick release method. Open the lid carefully. Remove the cake pan from the pot and let it cool for 20 minutes. Cut cake into slices and serve.

Nutrition: Calories 275 / Fat 25.5 g / Carbohydrates: 7.5 g

130. LEMON CHEESECAKE

Preparation time: 10 minutes - Cooking time: 35 minutes - Servings: 8

Ingredients: For crust: 2 tablespoon coconut oil, melted - 2 tablespoon swerve ¾ cup almond flour - pinch of salt - For filling: 2 tablespoon heavy whipping cream 2 large eggs - 1 teaspoon lemon extract - 1 teaspoon lemon zest - 4 tablespoons fresh lemon juice - 2/3 cup Swerve - 1 lb. cream cheese, softened

Directions: Grease a 7-inch spring-form pan with butter and line with parchment paper. Set aside. In a bowl, combine together all the crust ingredients and pour into the prepared pan and spread evenly, and place in the refrigerator for 15 minutes. In a large mixing bowl, beat cream cheese using a hand mixer until smooth. Add swerve, lemon extract, lemon zest, and lemon juice and beat again until just combined. Add eggs and heavy whipping cream and beat until well combined. Pour the filling mixture over the crust and spread evenly. Cover the springform pan with foil. Pour 1 cup of water into the instant pot, then place a trivet in the pot. Place cake pan on top of the trivet. Seal instant pot with the lid and select manual high pressure for 35 minutes. Allow releasing pressure naturally, then open the lid. Remove the cake pan from the pot and let it cool completely. Place in refrigerator for 3-4 hours. Serve chilled and enjoy.

Nutrition: Calories: 322 / Fat: 31.1 g / Carbohydrates: 4.4 g / Protein: 8.3 g

SAVORY BREAD

131. CREAM CHEESE BREAD

Preparation time: 10 minutes - Cooking time: 4 hours - Servings: 12 slices

Ingredients : ¼ cup butter, unsalted - 1 cup and 3 tbsp. cream cheese, softened
4 egg yolks - 1 tsp. vanilla extract - 1 tsp. baking powder - ¼ tsp. sea salt
2 tbsp. monk fruit powder - ½ cup peanut flour

Directions : Add butter and cream cheese until combined. Then beat in egg yolks, vanilla, baking powder, salt, and monk fruit powder and mix well. Add the egg mixture into the bread bucket. Top with flour and shut the lid. Select the Basic/white cycle or low-carb setting and press Start. Remove the bread when done. Cool, slice, and serve.

Nutrition: Calories: 98 / Fat: 7.9 g / Carb: 2.2 g / Protein: 3.5 g

132. LEMON POPPY SEED BREAD

Preparation time: 10 minutes - Cooking time: 4 hours - Servings: 6

Ingredients : 3 eggs - 1 ½ tbsp. butter, unsalted and melted - 1 ½ tbsp. lemon juice
1 lemon, zested - 1 ½ cups almond flour - ¼ cup erythritol sweetener
¼ tsp. baking powder - 1 tbsp. poppy seeds

Directions : Beat eggs, butter, lemon juice, and lemon zest until combined. In another bowl, add flour, sweetener, baking powder, and poppy seeds and mix well. Add the egg mixture into the bread pan, top with flour mixture, and cover. Select the Basic/White cycle or low-car setting and press Start. Remove the bread when done. Cool, slice, and serve.

Nutrition: Calories: 201 / Fat: 17.5 g / Carb: 2.8 g / Protein: 8.2 g

133. CAULIFLOWER AND GARLIC BREAD

Preparation time: 10 minutes - Cooking time: 4 hours - Servings: 9

Ingredients : 5 eggs, separated - 2/3 cup coconut flour - 1 1/2 cup rice cauliflower
1 tsp. minced garlic - ½ tsp. sea salt - ½ tbsp. chopped rosemary - ½ tbsp. chopped parsley
¾ tbsp. baking powder - 3 tbsp. butter, unsalted

Directions : Place the cauliflower rice in a bowl and cover it. Microwave for 3 to 4 minutes or until steamed. Then drain. Wrap in a cheesecloth and remove as much moisture as possible. Set aside. Place egg whites in a bowl and whisk until stiff peaks form. Then transfer ¼ of the whipped egg whites into a food processor. Add remaining ingredients except for cauliflower and pulse for 2 minutes until blended. Add cauliflower rice, and pulse for 2 minutes until combined. Then pulse in remaining egg whites until just mixed. Add batter into the bread bucket and cover. Select the Basic/white cycle or low-carb. Press Start. Remove the bread when done. Cool, slice, and serve.

Nutrition: Calories: 108 / Fat: 8 g / Carb: 3 g / Protein: 6 g

134. ALMOND MEAL BREAD

Preparation time: 10 minutes - Cooking time: 4 hours - Servings: 10 slices

Ingredients : 4 eggs - ¼ cup melted coconut oil - 1 tbsp. apple cider vinegar
2 ¼ cups almond meal - 1 tsp. baking soda - ¼ cup ground flaxseed meal
1 tsp. onion powder - 1 tbsp. minced garlic - 1 tsp. sea salt - 1 tsp. chopped sage leaves
1 tsp. fresh thyme - 1 tsp. chopped rosemary leaves

Directions : In a bowl, beat eggs, coconut oil, and vinegar until mixed. In another bowl, place an almond meal and add the remaining ingredients. Mix well. Add the egg mixture into the bread bucket, and top with flour mixture. Cover the lid. Select the Basic/White cycle or low-carb. Press Start. Remove the bread when done. Cool, slice, and serve.

Nutrition: Calories: 104 / Fat: 8.8 g / Carb: 2.1 g / Protein: 4 g

135. 3-SEED BREAD

Preparation time: 10 minutes - Cooking time: 4 hours - Servings: 18 slices

Ingredients : 2 eggs - ¼ cup butter, melted - 1 cup warm water (100F) - ¼ cup chia seeds
½ cup pumpkin seeds - ½ cup psyllium husks - ½ cup sunflower seeds - ¼ cup coconut flour
¼ tsp. salt - 1 tsp. baking powder

Directions : Beat eggs and butter in a bowl until well blended. Add flour to another bowl. Then stir in the remaining ingredients except for water until mixed. Pour water into the bread bucket, add egg mixture, and top with flour mixture. Cover. Select the Basic/White cycle or low-carb. Press Start. Remove the bread when done. Cool, slice, and serve.

Nutrition: Calories: 139 / Fat: 10 g / Carb: 5.6 g / Protein: 5 g

136. CHEESY GARLIC BREAD

Preparation time: 10 minutes - Cooking time: 4 hours - Servings: 16 slices

Ingredients : 5 eggs - 2 cups almond flour - ½ tsp. xanthan gum - 1 tsp. garlic powder
1 tsp. salt - 1 tsp. parsley - 1 tsp. Italian seasoning - 1 tsp. dried oregano - 1 stick of butter, unsalted and melted - 1 cup grated mozzarella cheese - 2 tbsp. ricotta cheese - 1 cup, grated cheddar cheese - 1/3 cup grated parmesan cheese
For topping : ½ stick butter, unsalted and melted - 1 tsp. garlic powder

Directions : Whisk the eggs in a bowl. Place flour in another bowl. Stir in xanthan gum and all the cheeses until well combined. Place butter in a bowl and add all the seasonings to it. Mix well. Add the egg mixture into the bread bucket. Then add the seasoning mixture and flour mixture. Cover. Select the Basic/white cycle or low-carb setting. Press Start. Remove the bread when done. Cool, slice, and serve.

Nutrition: Calories: 250 / Fat: 14.5 g / Carb: 1.4 g / Protein: 7.2 g

137. CUMIN BREAD

Preparation time: 10 minutes - Cooking time: 4 hours - Servings: 12 slices

Ingredients : 2 eggs - 1 ½ tbsp. avocado oil - 2/3 cup coconut milk, unsweetened
2 tbsp. Picante sauce - 1 cup almond flour - ½ cup coconut flour - ¼ tsp. salt
1 tbsp. baking powder - ¼ tsp. mustard powder - 2 tsp. ground cumin

Directions : Beat eggs until frothy, then beat in oil, milk, and sauce until combined. In another bowl, place flours, then stir in remaining ingredients and mix. Add egg mixture into the bread bucket, top with flour mixture, then cover. Select the Basic/White cycle or low-carb. Press Start. Remove the bread when done. Cool, slices, and serve.

Nutrition: Calories: 108 / Fat: 8.3 g / Carb: 4 g / Protein: 3.7 g

138. SESAME AND FLAX SEED BREAD

Preparation time: 10 minutes - Cooking time: 4 minutes - Servings: 10 slices

Ingredients : 3 eggs - ½ cup cream cheese, softened - 6 ½ tbsp. heavy whipping cream
¼ cup melted coconut oil - ½ cup almond flour - ¼ cup flaxseed - 6 ½ tbsp. coconut flour
2 2/3 tbsp. sesame seeds - ½ tsp. salt - 1 ½ tsp. baking powder - 2 tbsp. ground psyllium husk powder - ½ tsp. ground caraway seeds

Directions : Beat the eggs, cream cheese, whipping cream, and coconut oil until mixed. Add flours in another bowl. Then stir in remaining ingredients and mix. Add egg mixture into the bread bucket, then top with flour mixture. Cover. Select the Basic/White cycle or low-carb. Press Start. Remove the bread when done. Cool, slice, and serve.

Nutrition: Calories: 230 / Fat: 21 g / Carb: 6.2 g / Protein: 6.3 g

139. BACON AND CHEDDAR BREAD

Preparation time: 10 minutes - Cooking time: 4 hours - Servings: 9 slices

Ingredients : 2 eggs - ¼ cup beer - 2 tbsp. butter, unsalted and melted - ¼ cup bacon, cooked and crumbled - ½ cup shredded cheddar cheese - ½ tbsp. coconut flour - 1 cup almond flour
¼ tsp. salt - ½ tbsp. baking powder

Directions : Blend eggs, beer, and butter in a bowl. Fold in the bacon and cheese until just mixed. Add egg mixture into the bread bucket. Top with flour mixture (flour mixed with dry ingredients) and cover. Select the Basic/White cycle or low-carb and press Start. Remove the bread when done. Cool, slice, and serve.

Nutrition: Calories: 140 / Fat: 12 g / Carb: 3 g / Protein: 5 g

140. OLIVE BREAD

Preparation time: 10 minutes - Cooking time: 4 hours - Servings: 10 slices

Ingredients : 4 eggs - 4 tbsp. avocado oil - 1 tbsp. apple cider vinegar - ½ cup coconut flour 1 tbsp. baking powder - 2 tbsp. psyllium husk powder - 1 ½ tbsp. dried rosemary - ½ tsp. salt 1/3 cup black olives, chopped - ½ cup boiling water

Directions : Beat eggs, then blend in oil. Stir in vinegar and fold in the olives. In another bowl, place the flour, then stir in husk powder, baking powder, salt, and rosemary until mixed. Add egg mixture into the bread bucket, top with flour mixture, and cover. Select the Basic/White cycle or low-carb. Then press Start. Remove the bread when done. Cool, slice, and serve.

Nutrition: Calories: 85 / Fat: 6.5 g / Carb: 3.4 g / Protein: 2 g

141. JALAPEÑO CHEESE BREAD

Preparation time: 10 minutes - Cooking time: 4 hours - Servings: 8 slices

Ingredients : 2 tbsp. Greek yogurt, full-fat - 4 eggs - 1/3 cup coconut flour - ½ tsp. sea salt 2 tbsp. whole psyllium husks - 1 tsp. baking powder - ¼ cup diced, pickled jalapeños ¼ cup shredded cheddar cheese, divided

Directions : Beat yogurt and egg in a bowl. Place the flour in another bowl. Add the remaining ingredients and mix well. Add egg mixture into the bread bucket, top with flour mixture, and cover. Select the Basic/White cycle or low-carb and press Start. Remove the bread when done. Cool, slice, and serve.

Nutrition: Calories: 105 / Fat: 6.2 g / Carb: 3.4 g / Protein: 6.6 g

142. DILL AND CHEDDAR BREAD

Preparation time: 10 minutes - Cooking time: 4 hours - Servings: 10 slices

Ingredients : 4 eggs - ¼ tsp. cream of tarter - 5 tbsp. butter, unsalted - 2 cups grated cheddar cheese - 1 ½ cups almond flour - 1 scoop of egg white protein - ¼ tsp. salt - 1 tsp. garlic powder 4 tsp. baking powder - ¼ tbsp. dried dill weed

Directions : Beat eggs, cream of tartar, butter, and cheese until just mixed. Place flour in another bowl. Then stir in egg white protein, salt, garlic powder, baking powder, and dill and mix. Add the egg mixture into the bread bucket, top with flour mixture. Cover. Select the Basic/White cycle or low-carb and press Start. Remove the bread when done. Cool, slice, and serve.

Nutrition: Calories: 292 / Fat: 25.2 g / Carb: 6.1 g / Protein: 14.3 g

143. ITALIAN MOZZARELLA AND CREAM CHEESE BREAD

Preparation time: 10 minutes - Cooking time: 4 hours - Servings: 8 slices

Ingredients : ¾ cup shredded mozzarella cheese - ¼ cup cream cheese, softened - 1 egg
1/3 cup almond flour - ¼ tsp. garlic powder - 2 tsp. baking powder - ½ tsp. Italian seasoning
½ cup shredded cheddar cheese

Directions : Melt the mozzarella cheese and cream cheese in the microwave. Beat the egg in another bowl. Place flour in another bowl, add remaining ingredients, and mix. Add blended egg into the bread bucket, top with melted cheese mixture, and then with flour mixture.Cover. Select the Basic/White cycle or low-carb. Press Start. Remove the bread when done. Cool, slice, and serve.

Nutrition: Calories: 171 / Fat: 14.5 g / Carb: 1.5 g / Protein: 3.3 g

144. SOURDOUGH DOUGH

Preparation time: 10 minutes - Cooking time: 4 hours - Servings: 15

Ingredients : 2 eggs - 6 egg whites - ¾ cup coconut milk, unsweetened - ¼ cup apple cider vinegar - ½ cup of warm water (100F) - 1 ½ cups almond flour - ½ cup coconut flour
½ cup ground flaxseed - 1 tsp. salt - 1 tsp. baking soda - 1/3 cup psyllium powder

Directions : In a bowl, add eggs, egg white, milk, vinegar, and water and whisk until combined. In another bowl, place flour and stir in remaining ingredients until mixed. Add the egg mixture into the bread bucket, top with flour mixture, and cover. Select the Basic/White cycle or low-carb. Press Start. Remove the bread when done. Cool, slice, and serve.

Nutrition: Calories: 115 / Fat: 8 g / Carb: 4.7 g / Protein: 5 g

145. CHEDDAR AND HERB BREAD

Preparation time: 10 minutes - Cooking time: 4 hours - Servings: 16 slices

Ingredients : 6 eggs - ½ cup butter, unsalted, softened - 2 cups almond flour
1 tsp. baking powder - ½ tsp. xanthan gum - 2 tbsp. garlic powder - ½ tsp. salt
1 tbsp. dried parsley - ½ tbsp. dried oregano - 1 ½ cups shredded cheddar cheese

Directions : Beat eggs until frothy and then beat in the butter until combined. Place flour in another bowl. Stir in remaining ingredients until mixed. Add egg mixture into the bread bucket, top with flour mixture, and cover. Select the Basic/White cycle or low-carb and press Start. Remove the bread when done. Cool, slice, and serve.

Nutrition: Calories: 207 / Fat: 17.5 g / Carb: 5 g / Protein: 7.2 g

146. VEGETABLE LOAF

Preparation time: 10 minutes - Cooking time: 4 hours - Servings: 12 slices

Ingredients : 4 eggs - ¼ cup coconut oil - 1 medium grated zucchini - 1 cup grated pumpkin
1 small grated carrot - 1/3 cup coconut flour - 1 cup almond flour - 2 tbsp. pumpkin seeds
2 tbsp. flax seeds - 2 tbsp. sunflower seeds - 2 tbsp. sesame seeds - 2 tbsp. psyllium husks
2 tsp. salt - 1 tbsp. smoked paprika - 2 tsp. ground cumin - 2 tsp. baking powder

Directions : Beat the eggs until frothy, beat in the oil, and then stir in zucchini, pumpkin, and carrot until just mixed. Place flour in another bowl. Then stir in the remaining ingredients until mixed. Add egg mixture into the bread bucket, top with flour mixture, and cover. Select the Basic/White cycle or low-carb. Press Start. Remove the bread when done. Cool, slice, and serve.

Nutrition: Calories: 181 / Fat: 15 g / Carb: 6.6 g / Protein: 6.9 g

147. KETO ALMOND PUMPKIN QUICK BREAD

Preparation time: 10 minutes - Cooking time: 60 minutes - Servings: 16

Ingredients : 1/3 cup oil - 3 large eggs - 1 ½ cup pumpkin puree, canned - 1 cup granulated sugar - 1 ½ tsp. baking powder - ½ tsp. baking soda - ¼ tsp. salt - ¾ tsp. ground cinnamon
¼ tsp. ground nutmeg - ¼ tsp. ground ginger - 3 cups almond flour - ½ cup chopped pecans

Directions : Grease the bread machine pan with cooking spray. Mix all the wet ingredients in a bowl. Add all the dry ingredients except pecans until mixed. Pour the batter onto your bread machine pan and place it back inside the bread machine. Close and select Quick Bread. Add the pecans after the beep. Remove the bread when done. Cool, slice, and serve.

Nutrition: Calories: 54 / Fat: 13.3 g / Carb: 6.3 g / Protein: 9.6 g

148. KETO BASIL PARMESAN SLICES

Preparation time: 10 min - Cooking time: 3 hours and 25 min - Servings: 16 slices

Ingredients : 1 cup water - ½ cup parmesan cheese, grated - 3 tbsp. granulated sugar
1 tbsp. dried basil - 1 ½ tbsp. olive oil - 1 tsp. salt - 3 cups almond flour - 2 tsp. active dry yeast

Directions : Place everything in the bread machine according to bread machine recommendation. Select Basic and press Start. Remove the bread when done. Cool, slice, serve.

Nutrition: Calories: 96 / Fat: 8 g / Carb: 7 g / Protein: 6 g

149. KETO BLT WITH OOPSIE BREAD

Preparation time: 20 minutes - Cooking time: 25 minutes - Servings: 4

Ingredients: Eggs- 3 / Cream cheese- 4 and half oz. / Salt- a pinch
Psyllium husk powder- ½ tablespoon / Baking powder- ½ teaspoon
Mayonnaise- 8 tablespoons / Bacon- 5 oz. / Lettuce- 2 oz. / Sliced tomato- 1 / Basil- a few

Directions: Preheat your oven at 300 degrees Fahrenheit. Separate the egg yolks and the egg whites. Beat the egg whites with the salt until the soft foaming mixture emerges. Mix the cream cheese with the egg yolks. Now mix in the baking powder and the psyllium husk powder. Now fold the egg whites in the egg yolk mixture. Put the oopsies on a greased baking tray. Put it to bake in preheated oven for 25 minutes or until they turn golden brown. For the BLT, fry the bacon pieces until they turn crispy. Spread the mayonnaise on the oopsie bread. Now place over the lettuce, sliced tomatoes and chopped basil on top. Finally put over the fried bacon pieces. Serve!

Nutrition: Calories: 346 / Fat: 31.26 g / Carb: 4.44 g / Protein: 12.81 g

150. OOPSIE ROLLS

Preparation time: 20 minutes - Cooking time: 30 minutes - Servings: 6

Ingredients: Eggs- 3 / Cream of tartar- 1/8 teaspoon / Cream cheese- 3 oz. / Salt- 1/8 teasp.

Directions: Preheat your oven at 300 degrees Fahrenheit. Separate the egg yolks and the egg whites. Whip the egg whites with the cream of tartar until soft peaks form. Now in another bowl mix the egg yolks, cream cheese and the salt. Now fold the egg whites in to the egg yolk mixture. Pour the batter on to a greased pan and put to bake in preheated oven for 30 minutes. Cool for a few minutes and then serve!

Nutrition: Calories: 109 / Fat: 9.13 g / Carb: 1.04 g / Protein: 5.55 g

151. COCONUT FLOUR FLATBREAD

Preparation time: 20 minutes - Cooking time: 30 minutes - Servings: 8

Ingredients: Egg- 1 / Coconut flour- 1 tablespoon / Parmesan cheese- 1 tablespoon
Baking soda- 1/8 teaspoon / Baking powder- 1/8 teaspoon / Salt- ¼ teaspoon
Butter- 2 tablespoons / Milk- 2 tablespoons

Directions: Mix together the coconut flour, baking soda, baking powder and the salt together, Now mix in the egg and the milk. Mix the mixture properly. Melt butter in a pan and pour in the batter to fry just like a pancake. Flip to the other side when one side is fried. Sprinkle over the parmesan cheese. Repeat with the remaining mixture. Serve!

Nutrition: Calories: 109 / Fat: 9.13 g / Carb: 1.04 g / Protein: 5.55 g

152. ALMOND BUNS

Preparation time: 5 minutes - Cooking time: 17 minutes - Servings: 3

Ingredients: Almond flour- ¾ cup / Eggs- 2 / Butter- 5 tablespoons / Splenda- 1.5 tablespoon Baking powder- 1.5 teaspoon

Directions: Mix together the sweetener, Splenda, baking powder and the almond flour. Now mix in the eggs. Now melt the butter and put in the mixture. Pour the mixture equally in to greased muffin cups. Preheat your oven at 350 degrees Fahrenheit. Put the muffin tray in the preheated oven to bake for 15 to 17 minutes or until done. Serve when cool!

Nutrition: Calories: 207 / Fat: 19.43 g / Carb: 0.74 g / Protein: 6.81 g

153. COCONUT AND ALMOND BREAD

Preparation time: 10 minutes - Cooking time: 30 minutes - Servings: 12

Ingredients: Almond flour- 1 ½ cups / Coconut flour- 2 tablespoons / Flaxseeds- ¼ cup Salt- ¼ teaspoon / Baking soda- 1 ½ teaspoon / Eggs- 5 / Coconut oil- ¼ cup Sweetener- 1 teaspoon / Apple cider vinegar- 1 tablespoon

Directions: Preheat your oven at 350 degrees Fahrenheit. Mix together the dry ingredients; almond flour, coconut flour, flax seeds, sweetener, salt and the baking soda. Now add in the eggs, coconut oil and the apple cider vinegar. Pour the batter in to a greased loaf pan and then put to bake in preheated oven for 30 minutes or until done. Cool it and then serve!

Nutrition: Calories: 207 / Fat: 19.43 g / Carb: 0.74 g / Protein: 6.81 g

154. QUICK COCONUT FLATBREAD

Preparation time: 10 minutes - Cooking time: 1 hour - Servings: 2

Ingredients: Eggs- 2 / Cream cheese- 2 oz. / Almond flour-1 tablespoon Cinnamon- 1 teaspoon / Erythritol-½ tablespoon / Salt- a pinch /Shredded coconut- ¼ cup Maple syrup- 4 tablespoons

Directions: Beat together the eggs in a bowl and then add in the cream cheese and the almond flour. In the mixture, add in the cinnamon, erythritol and the salt. Mix properly and then pour some of the batter in to a frying pan and fry the on both sides properly. Put in to a plate and sprinkle over the shredded coconut and then the maple syrup. Enjoy!

Nutrition: Calories: 334 / Fat: 18.62 g / Carb: 31.17 g / Protein: 11.51 g

155. 5 INGREDIENT CHOCOLATE CHIP KETO BREAD

Preparation time: 8 minutes - Cooking time: 25 minutes - Servings: 2

Ingredients: Protein powder- 2 scoops / Eggs, separated- 2 / Butter- 2 tablespoons
Salt- a pinch / Cacao nibs- 50 grams / Maple syrup- ½ cup

Directions: Beat the egg whites until stiff peaks form. In another bowl, mix the egg yolks, protein powder and the butter. Now fold in the egg whites in to this mixture. Now add in the salt and the cacao nibs. Mix well. Preheat your oven at 350 degrees Fahrenheit. Pour this mixture in to a greased cake pan and bake until it turns golden brown for approximately 25 minutes. Serve warm and drizzle over maple syrup!

Nutrition: Calories: 505 / Fat: 20.04 g / Carb: 59.31 g / Protein: 21.96 g

156. PEANUT BUTTER AND CHOCOLATE BREAD

Preparation time: 20 minutes - Cooking time: 25 minutes - Servings: 6

Ingredients: Almond flour- 1 cup / Erythritol- ½ cup / Baking powder- 1 teaspoon
Salt- a pinch / Peanut butter- 1/3 cup / Almond milk-1/3 cup / Eggs- 2 / Cacao nibs- ½ cup

Directions: Mix together the almond flour, erythritol, baking powder and the salt. Now add in the peanut butter, almond milk and the eggs. Mix well. Lastly fold in the cacao nibs and put the mixture in to a prepared greased pan. Preheat your oven at 350 degrees Fahrenheit and put the pan to bake in the preheated oven for 25 minutes or until the cake is cooked. Serve and enjoy!

Nutrition: Calories: 107 / Fat: 7.3 g / Carb: 4.51 g / Protein: 5.52 g

157. EASY BLENDER FLATBREAD WITH A TOUCH OF CINNAMON

Preparation time: 5 minutes - Cooking time: 14 minutes - Servings: 4

Ingredients: Cream cheese- 2 oz. / Eggs- 2 / Protein powder- 1 scoop / Cinnamon- a pinch
Coconut oil- 1 tablespoon / Salt- a pinch

Directions: Take a blender and blend in the cream cheese, eggs, protein powder, cinnamon and the salt. Heat up a frying pan with coconut oil and put in the batter to fry. Cook the flatbread on both sides. Serve when done!

Nutrition: Calories: 163 / Fat: 13.26 g / Carb: 2.41 g / Protein: 8.67 g

158. LOW CARB VANILLA BREAD

Preparation time: 10 minutes - Cooking time: 30 minutes - Servings: 5

Ingredients: Eggs, separated- 5 / Coconut flour- 4tbsp / Granulated sweetener- 4tbsp
Baking powder- 1tsp / Vanilla extract- 2tsp / Full fat milk- 3tbsp / Melted butter- 125 grams

Directions: Separate the egg whites and the egg yolks and beat the egg whites until they form in to stiff peaks. In another bowl, beat the egg yolks, coconut flour, granulated sweetener and the baking powder. Now slowly and gradually pour in the melted butter carefully and mix it to make sure that you have a very smooth consistency of your batter. Now add in the full fat milk and the vanilla extract. With the help of a rubber spatula, now very gently fold in the egg whites in the mixture. Try to keep as much as air and fluffiness that you can for better results. Preheat your oven at 350 degrees Fahrenheit and put the pan to bake in preheated oven for 30 minutes or until it is golden brown. Cool and then serve!

Nutrition: Calories: 175 / Fat: 9.89 g / Carb: 10.51 g / Protein: 9.37 g

159. VERY YUMMY CHOCOLATE BREAD

Preparation time: 5 minutes - Cooking time: 15 minutes - Servings: 1

Ingredients: Cocoa powder- 2 tablespoons / Almond flour- ½ cup / Erythritol- 2 tablespoons
Egg- 1 / Heavy cream- 1 tablespoon / Vanilla extract- ½ teaspoon / Baking powder- ¼ teaspoon
Salt-a pinch

Directions: Preheat your oven at 350 degrees Fahrenheit. Whisk together the cocoa powder, almond flour and the sweetener erythritol and make sure to remove lumps. In another bowl, beat the egg well. Now add the egg, heavy cream and the vanilla extract in to the erythritol mixture and mix. Add in the salt and baking powder as well. Mix all the ingredients properly. Grease your pan, pour the batter in and then put it to bake in preheated oven for 10 to 15 minutes or until the bread is done. Serve while the bread cool down.

Nutrition: Calories: 139 / Fat: 11.55 g / Carb: 1.55 g / Protein: 7.1 g

160. WHOLE GRAIN BREAD

Preparation time: 10 minutes - Cooking time: 40-45 minutes - Servings: 6

Ingredients: Eggs- 2 / Skim milk- 1 ¾ cups / Canola oil- ¼ cup / Applesauce- ¼ cup
Vanilla extract- 1 teaspoon / Pastry flour- 1 cup / Flax seed meal- ½ cup / Wheat germ- ¼ cup
Flour- ¼ cup / Baking powder- 4 teaspoons / Sugar- 1 tablespoon / Salt- ¼ teaspoon

Directions: Preheat your oven at 350 degrees Fahrenheit. In a bowl, first mix the wet ingredients such as the eggs, skim milk, canola oil, applesauce, vanilla extract with the dry ones that are pastry flour, flax seed meal and the wheat germ. Now mix in the flour, baking powder, sugar and salt. Pour the batter in to the prepared pan and bake until the bread turns golden brown. Cool and serve!

Nutrition: Calories: 234 / Fat: 13.9 g / Carb: 19.41 g / Protein: 7.98 g

161. CHEDDAR AND CHIVE BREAD

Preparation time: 15 minutes - Cooking time: 25 minutes - Servings: 8

Ingredients: Almond flour- ½ cup / Salt- 1 teaspoon / Ground mustard- 1 teaspoon
Black pepper- 1 teaspoon / Xanthan gum- ½ teaspoon / Cayenne pepper- ¼ teaspoon
Heavy cream- ¾ cup / Shredded cheddar cheese- 2 cups / Chopped chives- ¼ cup
Eggs- 6 / Cream of tartar- ¼ teaspoon / Salt- a pinch

Directions: Preheat your oven at 350 degrees Fahrenheit. Grease your loaf tin. In a bowl, mix together the almond flour, salt, ground mustard, black pepper, xanthan gum, cayenne pepper with heavy cream and the shredded cheddar cheese. Now mix in the chopped fresh chives. Make sure that the ingredients are mixed properly. Separate the egg yolks and the egg whites and mix in the egg yolks in the mixture. In another bowl, beat the egg whites and the cream of tartar until stiff peaks form. Add a pinch of salt. Fold the egg whites in to the egg yolk mixture to incorporate well. Pour the mixture in to a greased loaf pan and put them to bake in preheated oven for 20 to 25 minutes or until the bread rises and turns golden brown. Serve hot immediately!

Nutrition: Calories: 175 / Fat: 9.89 g / Carb: 10.51 g / Protein: 9.37 g

162. GRAIN FREE CASHEW SOURDOUGH BREAD

Preparation time: 30 minutes - Cooking time: 50 minutes - Servings: 12

Ingredients: Cashews- 10 / Water- 4 ounces / Probiotic capsules- equal to 30-40 billion strains / Eggs, separated- 2 / Water- 1 tablespoon / Baking soda- ½ teaspoon
Salt- ¼ teaspoon / Egg yolk plus water 1 tablespoon

Directions: Blend the cashews with filtered water. Put the mixture in to a bowl, add in the probiotic capsules and then mix them well. Cover the bowl and put in the oven which should not be more than 110 degrees for 12 hours at least. The longer you let it sit the more sour it will become. When it is ready, preheat the oven on 325 degrees. Put the cashew mixture in to a bowl. Separate both the egg yolks and the egg whites and add the egg yolks in the cashew mixture with the water. Now add the baking soda and salt in the cashew mixture. Beat the egg whites until soft peaks form and then fold them in the egg yolks and cashew mixture. Pour the mixture in to a prepared loaf tin. Mix the egg yolk and the water and use the pastry brush for the egg wash. Bake at 325 degrees for 50 minutes. Serve when cool.

Nutrition: Calories: 23 / Fat: 1.62 g / Carb: 0.49 g / Protein: 1.5 g

163. WHOLE WHEAT COCONUT BREAD

Preparation time: 10 minutes - Cooking time: 25 minutes - Servings: 8

Ingredients: Pastry flour- 1 ½ cups / Sugar- 2 tablespoons / Baking powder- 2 teaspoons
Salt- ½ teaspoon / Milk- 1 ½ cups / Melted coconut oil- 1/3 cup / Egg- 1
Vanilla extract- ½ teaspoon

Directions: Preheat your oven at 350 degrees Fahrenheit. Mix together the pastry flour, sugar, baking powder and salt. Make a well in the center and add in the wet ingredients that are milk, melted coconut oil, egg and vanilla extract. Pour the batter in to a greased cake pan and cook until the bread turns golden brown for approximately 25 minutes. Cool and serve!

Nutrition: Calories: 152 / Fat: 11.98 g / Carb: 8.72 g / Protein: 3.03 g

164. KETO BLUEBERRY LEMON BREAD

Preparation time: 30 minutes - Cooking time: 50 minutes - Servings: 16

Ingredients: Almond flour- 3 cups / Egg white protein powder- 2 tablespoons
Cream of tartar- 1 teaspoon / Baking soda- ½ teaspoon / Celtic sea salt- ¼ teaspoon
Eggs- 6 / Lemon zest- 1 tablespoon / Vanilla extract- ½ tablespoon
Vanilla stevia- ½ teaspoon Blue berries- 1 cup

Directions: In a food processor, blend together the almond flour, egg white protein powder, cream of tartar, baking soda and the salt. Now add in the eggs, lemon zest, vanilla extract and the vanilla stevia. Now fold in the blue berries. Mix the batter well and then pour the batter in to a prepared greased pan. Preheat your oven at 350 degrees Fahrenheit. Put the pan to bake in preheated oven for 45 to 50 minutes or until baked to perfection. Cool and then serve!

Nutrition: Calories: 85 / Fat: 6.22 g / Carb: 0.81 g / Protein: 5.95 g

165. EASY LOW CARB BAKED BREAD

Preparation time: 15 minutes - Cooking time: 10 minutes - Servings: 12

Ingredients: Almond flour- 2 ½ cups / Baking powder- 2 teaspoons
Baking soda- ¼ teaspoon / Salt- ¼ teaspoon / Softened butter- ¼ cup
Egg white protein powder- 2 tablespoon Eggs- 3 / Anise extract- 4 teaspoons

Directions: Preheat your oven at 350 degrees Fahrenheit. Mix almond flour, baking powder, baking soda and salt in a bowl. In a separate bowl, beat the butter. Now add in the eggs, anise extract and beat them with butter. Now mix in the flour and the egg white protein powder and form the dough. Cut the dough lengthwise and place the slices on to a prepared baking sheet. Put the slices to bake in preheated oven for about 10 minutes or until both sides turn brown. Cool and serve!

Nutrition: Calories: 75 / Fat: 6.49 g / Carb: 0.71 g / Protein: 3.42 g

PROTEIN BREAD

166. CHIA SEED BREAD

Preparation time: 10 minutes - Cooking time: 40 minutes - Servings: 16 slices

Ingredients: ½ tsp. xanthan gum - ½ cup butter - 2 Tbsp. coconut oil - 1 Tbsp. baking powder
3 Tbsp. sesame seeds - 2 Tbsp. chia seeds - ½ tsp. salt - ¼ cup sunflower seeds
2 cups almond flour - 7 eggs

Directions: Preheat the oven to 350F. Beat eggs in a bowl on high for 1 to 2 minutes. Beat in the xanthan gum and combine coconut oil and melted butter into eggs, beating continuously. Set aside the sesame seeds, but add the rest of the ingredients. Line a loaf pan with baking paper and place the mixture in it. Top the mixture with sesame seeds. Bake in the oven until a toothpick inserted comes out clean, about 35 to 40 minutes.

Nutrition: Calories: 405 / Fat: 37 g / Carb: 4 g / Protein: 14 g

167. KETO FLAX BREAD

Preparation time: 10 minutes - Cooking time: 18 to 20 minutes - Servings: 8

Ingredients: ¾ cup of water - 200 g ground flax seeds - ½ cup psyllium husk powder
1 Tbsp. baking powder - 7 large egg whites - 3 Tbsp. butter - 2 tsp. salt - ¼ cup granulated stevia
1 large whole egg - 1 ½ cups whey protein isolate

Directions: Preheat the oven to 350F. Combine together whey protein isolate, psyllium husk, baking powder, sweetener, and salt. In another bowl, mix together the water, butter, egg, and egg whites. Slowly add psyllium husk mixture to egg mixture and mix well. Lightly grease a bread pan with butter and pour in the batter. Bake in the oven until the bread is set, about 18 to 20 minutes.

Nutrition: Calories: 265.5 / Fat: 15.68 g / Carb: 1.88 g / Protein: 24.34 g

168. SPECIAL KETO BREAD

Preparation time: 15 minutes - Cooking time: 40 minutes - Servings: 14

Ingredients: 2 tsp. baking powder - ½ cup water - 1 Tbsp. poppy seeds - 2 cups fine ground almond meal - 5 large eggs - ½ cup olive oil - ½ tsp. fine Himalayan salt

Directions: Preheat the oven to 400F. In a bowl, combine salt, almond meal, and baking powder. Drip in oil while mixing, until it forms a crumbly dough. Make a little round hole in the middle of the dough and pour eggs into the middle of the dough. Pour water and whisk eggs together with the mixer in the small circle until it is frothy. Start making larger circles to combine the almond meal mixture with the dough until you have a smooth and thick batter. Line your loaf pan with parchment paper. Pour batter into the prepared loaf pan and sprinkle poppy seeds on top. Bake in the oven for 40 minutes in the center rack until firm and golden brown. Cool in the oven for 30 minutes. Slice and serve.

Nutrition: Calories: 227 / Fat: 21 g / Carb: 4 g / Protein: 7 g

169. KETO EASY BREAD

Preparation time: 15 minutes - Cooking time: 45 minutes - Servings: 10

Ingredients: ¼ tsp. cream of tartar - 1 ½ tsp. baking powder (double acting) - 4 large eggs 1 ½ cups vanilla whey protein - ¼ cup olive oil - ¼ cup coconut milk, unsweetened ½ tsp. salt - ¼ cup unsalted butter, softened - 12 oz. cream cheese, softened ½ tsp. xanthan gum - ½ tsp. baking soda

Directions : Preheat oven to 325F. Layer aluminum foil over the loaf pan and spray with olive oil. Beat the butter with cream cheese in a bowl until mixed well. Add oil and coconut milk and blend until mixed. Add eggs, one by one until fully mixed. Set aside. In a bowl, whisk whey protein, ½ tsp. xanthan gum, baking soda, cream of tartar, salt, and baking powder. Add mixture to egg/cheese mixture and slowly mix until fully combined. Don't over blend. Place in the oven and bake for 40 to 45 minutes, or until golden brown. Cool, slice, and serve.

Nutrition: Calories: 294.2 / Fat: 24 g / Carb: 1.8 g / Protein: 17 g

170. ALMOND FLOUR APPLE BREAD ROLLS

Preparation time: 10 minutes - Cooking time: 30 minutes - Servings: 6

Ingredients: 1 cup boiling water or as needed - 2 cups almond flour - ½ cup ground flaxseed 4 Tbsp. psyllium husk powder - 1 Tbsp. baking powder - 2 Tbsp. olive oil - 2 eggs 1 Tbsp. apple cider vinegar - ½ tsp. salt

Directions: Preheat the oven to 350F. In a bowl, mix together the almond flour, baking powder, psyllium husk powder, flax-seed flour, and salt. Add the olive oil and eggs and blend until mixture resembles breadcrumbs, then mix in the apple cider vinegar. Slowly add boiling water and mix into the mixture. Let stand for half an hour to firm up. Line parchment paper over the baking tray. Using your hands, make a ball of the dough. Transfer dough balls on a baking tray and bake for 30 minutes, or until firm and golden.

Nutrition: Calories: 301 / Fat: 24.1 g / Carb: 5 g / Protein: 11 g

171. BREAD DE SOUL

Preparation time: 10 minutes - Cooking time: 45 minutes - Servings: 16

Ingredients: ¼ tsp. cream of tartar - 2 ½ tsp. baking powder - 1 tsp. xanthan gum 1/3 tsp. baking soda - ½ tsp. salt - 1 2/3 cup unflavored whey protein - ¼ cup olive oil ¼ cup heavy whipping cream or half and half - 2 drops of sweet leaf stevia - 4 eggs ¼ cup butter - 12 oz. softened cream cheese

Directions: Preheat the oven to 325F. In a bowl, microwave cream cheese and butter for 1 minute. Remove and blend well with a hand mixer. Add olive oil, eggs, heavy cream, and few drops of sweetener and blend well. Blend together the dry ingredients in a separate bowl. Combine the dry ingredients with the wet ingredients and mix with a spoon. Don't use a hand blender to avoid whipping it too much. Grease a bread pan and pour the mixture into the pan. Bake in the oven until golden brown, about 45 minutes. Cool and serve.

Nutrition: Calories: 200 / Fat: 15.2 g / Carb: 1.8 g / Protein: 10 g

172. SANDWICH FLATBREAD

Preparation time: 15 minutes - Cooking time: 20 minutes - Servings: 10

Ingredients: ¼ cup water - ¼ cup oil - 4 eggs - ½ tsp. salt - 1/3 cup unflavored whey protein powder - ½ tsp. garlic powder - 2 tsp. baking powder - 6 Tbsp. coconut flour - 3 ¼ cups almond flour

Directions: Preheat the oven to 325F. Combine the dry ingredients in a large bowl and mix with a hand whisk. Whisk in eggs, oil, and water until combined well. Place on a piece of large parchment paper and flatten into a rough rectangle. Place another parchment paper on top. Roll into a large ½ inch to ¾ inch thick rough rectangle. Transfer to the baking sheet and discard the parchment paper on top. Bake until it is firm to the touch, about 20 minutes. Cool and cut into 10 portions. Carefully cut each part into two halves through the bready center. Stuff with your sandwich fillings. Serve.

Nutrition: Calories: 316 / Fat: 6.8 g / Carb: 11 g / Protein: 25.9 g

173. KETO SANDWICH BREAD

Preparation time: 5 minutes - Cooking time: 1 hour - Servings: 12

Ingredients: 1 tsp. apple cider vinegar - ¾ cup water - ¼ cup avocado oil - 5 eggs
½ tsp. salt - 1 tsp. baking soda - ½ cup coconut flour - 2 cups plus 2 Tbsp. almond flour

Directions: Preheat the oven to 350F and grease a loaf pan. In a bowl, whisk almond flour, coconut flour, and salt. In another bowl, separate the egg whites from egg yolks. Set egg whites aside. In a blender, blend the oil, egg yolks, water, vinegar, and baking soda for 5 minutes on medium speed until combined. Let the mixture sit for 1 minute then add in the reserved egg whites and mix until frothy, about 10 to 15 seconds. Add the dry ingredients and process on high for 5 to 10 seconds before batter becomes too thick for the blender. Blend until the batter is smooth. Transfer batter into the greased loaf pan and smoothen the top. Bake in the oven until a skewer inserted comes out clean, about 50 to 70 minutes. Cool, slice, and serve.

Nutrition: Calories: 200 / Fat: 7 g / Carb: 7 g / Protein: 16 g

174. COCONUT FLOUR ALMOND BREAD

Preparation time: 10 minutes - Cooking time: 30 minutes - Servings: 4

Ingredients: 1 Tbsp. butter, melted - 1 Tbsp. coconut oil, melted - 6 eggs - 1 tsp. baking soda 2 Tbsp. ground flaxseed - 1 ½ Tbsp. psyllium husk powder - 5 Tbsp. coconut flour - 1 ½ cup almond flour

Directions: Preheat the oven to 400F. Mix the eggs in a bowl for a few minutes. Add in the butter and coconut oil and mix once more for 1 minute. Add the almond flour, coconut flour, baking soda, psyllium husk, and ground flaxseed to the mixture. Let sit for 15 minutes. Lightly grease the loaf pan with coconut oil. Pour the mixture in the pan. Place in the oven and bake until a toothpick inserted in it comes out dry, about 25 minutes.

Nutrition: Calories: 475 / Fat: 38 g / Carb: 7 g / Protein: 19 g

175. KETO CLOUD BREAD CHEESE

Preparation time: 5 minutes - Cooking time: 30 minutes - Servings: 12

Ingredients : for cream cheese filling: 1 egg yolk - ½ tsp. vanilla stevia drops for filling 8 oz. softened cream cheese - Base egg dough: ½ tsp. cream of tartar - 1 Tbsp. coconut flour ¼ cup unflavored whey protein - 3 oz. softened cream cheese - ¼ tsp. vanilla stevia drops for dough - 4 eggs, separated

Directions: Preheat the oven to 325F. Line two baking sheets with parchment paper. In a bowl, stir the 8 ounces cream cheese, stevia, and egg yolk. Transfer to the pastry bag. In another bowl, separate egg yolks from whites. Add 3 oz. cream cheese, yolks, stevia, whey protein, and coconut flour. Mix until smooth. Whip cream of tartar with the egg whites until stiff peaks form. Fold in the yolk/cream cheese mixture into the beaten whites. Spoon batter onto each baking sheet, 6 mounds on each. Press each mound to flatten a bit. Add cream cheese filling in the middle of each batter. Bake for 30 minutes at 325F.

Nutrition: Calories: 120 / Fat: 10.7 g / Carb: 1.1 g / Protein: 5.4 g

176. MY KETO BREAD

Preparation time: 10 minutes - Cooking time: 50 to 60 minutes - Servings: 6

Ingredients: 3 egg whites - 1 cup of boiling water - 2 Tbsp. sesame seeds - 2 tsp. cider vinegar 1 tsp. sea salt - 2 tsp. baking powder - 5 Tbsp. ground psyllium husk powder - 1 ¼ cups almond flour

Directions: Preheat the oven to 350F. Mix the dry ingredients in a bowl. In another bowl, add the boiling water, vinegar, and egg whites. Beat for 30 seconds with a hand mixer. Don't over mix. Grease hands with oil to make 6 pieces then arrange on a greased baking sheet. Bake 50 to 60 minutes in the lower rack of the oven. Cooking time depends on the size of the bread. The bread is ready when it makes a hollow sound when tapped.

Nutrition: Calories: 170 / Fat: 13 g / Carb: 2 g / Protein: 7 g

177. KETO OAT CORNBREAD

Preparation time: 10 minutes - Cooking time: 20 minutes - Servings: 8

Ingredients: ¼ tsp. corn extract - 4 eggs - ¼ cup water - 1/3 cup melted bacon fat or coconut oil - 4 oz. melted butter - ¼ tsp. salt - 1 ½ tsp. baking powder - 1/3 cup whey protein isolate, unflavored - ½ cup oat fiber - ¼ cup coconut flour

Directions: Preheat oven to 350F. Grease a 10-inch cast iron skillet and place in the oven to warm up. Combine all the dry ingredients in a bowl. Add the eggs, water, melted butter, and bacon fat. Beat with a hand mixer, then mix in corn extract. Transfer mixture into the heated skillet. Bake at 350F for 18 to 20 minutes or until firm and top is lightly browned.

Nutrition: Calories: 240 / Fat: 23 g / Carb: 1 g / Protein: 7 g

178. CHEESY KETO SESAME BREAD

Preparation time: 5 minutes - Cooking time: 30 minutes - Servings: 8

Ingredients: 1 tsp. sesame seeds - 1 tsp. baking powder - 1 tsp. salt - 2 Tbsp. ground psyllium husk powder - 1 cup almond flour - 4 Tbsp. sesame or olive oil - 7 ounces cream cheese - 4 eggs Sea salt

Directions: Preheat the oven to 400F. Beat the eggs until fluffy. Add cream cheese and oil until combined well. Set the sesame seeds aside and add the remaining ingredients. Grease a baking tray. Spread the dough in the greased baking tray. Allow it to stand for 5 minutes. Baste dough with oil and top with a sprinkle of sesame seeds and a little sea salt.Bake in the oven at 400F until the top is golden brown, about 30 minutes.

Nutrition: Calories: 282 / Fat: 26 g / Carb: 2 g / Protein: 7 g

179. BREAD WITH BEEF AND PEANUTS

Preparation time: 3 hours - Cooking time: 20 minutes - Servings: 8

Ingredients : 15 oz. beef meat - 5 oz. herbs de provence - 2 big onions - 2 cloves chopped garlic 1 cup of milk - 20 oz. almond flour - 10 oz. rye flour - 3 teaspoons dry yeast - 1 egg 3 tablespoons sunflower oil - 1 tablespoon sugar - Sea salt - Ground black pepper - Red pepper

Directions : Sprinkle the beef meat with the herbs de provence, salt, black, and red pepper and marinate in bear for overnight. Cube the beef and fry in a skillet or a wok on medium heat until soft (for around 20 minutes). Chop the onions and garlic and then fry them until clear and caramelized. Combine all the ingredients except for the beef and then mix well. Combine the beef pieces and the dough and mix in the bread machine. Close the lid and turn the bread machine on the basic program. Bake the bread until the medium crust and after the bread is ready take it out and leave for 1 hour covered with the towel and only then you can slice the bread.

Nutrition: Carbohydrates 4 g / Fats 42 g / Protein 27 g / Calories 369

180. BASIC SWEET YEAST BREAD

Preparation time: 3 hours - Cooking time: 20 minutes - Servings: 8

Ingredients : 1 egg - ¼ cup butter - 1/3 cup sugar - 1 cup milk - ½ teaspoon salt 4 cups almond flour - 1 tablespoon active dry yeast - After beeping: Fruits/ground nuts

Directions : Add all of the ingredients to your bread machine, carefully following the instructions of the manufacturer (except fruits/ground nuts). Set the program of your bread machine to basic/sweet and set crust type to light or medium. Press start. Once the machine beeps, add fruits/ground nuts. Wait until the cycle completes. Once the loaf is ready, take the bucket out and let the loaf cool for 5 minutes. Gently shake the bucket to remove loaf. Transfer to a cooling rack, slice and serve. Enjoy!

Nutrition: Carbohydrates 2.7 g / Fats 7.6 g / Protein 8.8 g / Calories 338

181. APRICOT PRUNE BREAD

Preparation time: 3 hours - Cooking time: 20 minutes - Servings: 8

Ingredients : 1 egg - 4/5 cup whole milk - ¼ cup apricot juice - ¼ cup butter - 1/5 cup sugar
4 cups almond flour - 1 tablespoon instant yeast - ¼ teaspoon salt - 5/8 cup prunes, chopped
5/8 cup dried apricots, chopped

Directions : Add all of the ingredients to your bread machine, carefully following the instructions of the manufacturer (except apricots and prunes). Set the program of your bread machine to basic/sweet and set crust type to light or medium. Press start. Once the machine beeps, add apricots and prunes. Wait until the cycle completes. Once the loaf is ready, take the bucket out and let the loaf cool for 5 minutes. Gently shake the bucket to remove loaf. Transfer to a cooling rack, slice and serve. Enjoy!

Nutrition: Carbohydrates 4 g / Fats 8.2 g / Protein 9 g / Calories 364

182. CITRUS BREAD

Preparation time: 3 hours - Cooking time: 1 hour - Servings: 8

Ingredients : 1 egg - 3 tablespoons butter - 1/3 cup sugar - 1 tablespoon vanilla sugar
½ cup orange juice - 2/3 cup milk - 1 teaspoon salt - 4 cup almond flour
1 tablespoon instant yeast - ¼ cup candied oranges - ¼ cup candied lemon
2 teaspoons lemon zest - ¼ cup almond, chopped

Directions : Add all of the ingredients to your bread machine, carefully following the instructions of the manufacturer (except candied fruits, zest, and almond). Set the program of your bread machine to basic/sweet and set crust type to light or medium. Press start. Once the machine beeps, add candied fruits, lemon zest, and chopped almonds. Wait until the cycle completes. Once the loaf is ready, take the bucket out and let the loaf cool for 5 minutes. Gently shake the bucket to remove loaf. Transfer to a cooling rack, slice and serve. Enjoy!

Nutrition: Carbohydrates 4 g / Fats 9.1 g / Protein 9.8 g / Calories 404

183. FRUIT BREAD

Preparation time: 3 hours - Cooking time: 40 minutes - Servings: 8

Ingredients : 1 egg - 1 cup milk - 2 tablespoons rum - ¼ cup butter - ¼ cup brown sugar
4 cups almond flour - 1 tablespoon instant yeast - 1 teaspoon salt
Fruits: ¼ cups dried apricots, coarsely chopped - ¼ cups prunes, coarsely chopped
¼ cups candied cherry, pitted - ½ cups seedless raisins - ¼ cup almonds, chopped

Directions : Add all of the ingredients to your bread machine, carefully following the instructions of the manufacturer (except fruits). Set the program of your bread machine to basic/sweet and set crust type to light or medium. Press start. Once the machine beeps, add fruits. Wait until the cycle completes. Once the loaf is ready, take the bucket out and let the loaf cool for 5 minutes. Gently shake the bucket to remove loaf. Transfer to a cooling rack, slice and serve.

Nutrition: Carbohydrates 5 g / Fats 10.9 g / Protein 10.8 g / Calories 441

184. MARZIPAN CHERRY BREAD

Preparation time: 3 hours - Cooking time: 35 minutes - Servings: 8

Ingredients : 1 egg - ¾ cup milk - 1 tablespoon almond liqueur - 4 tablespoons orange juice ½ cup ground almonds - ¼ cup butter - 1/3 cup sugar - 4 cups almond flour - 1 tablespoon instant yeast - 1 teaspoon salt - ½ cup marzipan - ½ cup dried cherries, pitted

Directions : Add all of the ingredients to your bread machine, carefully following the instructions of the manufacturer (except marzipan and cherry). Set the program of your bread machine to basic/sweet and set crust type to light or medium. Press start. Once the machine beeps, add marzipan and cherry. Wait until the cycle completes. Once the loaf is ready, take the bucket out and let the loaf cool for 5 minutes. Gently shake the bucket to remove loaf. Transfer to a cooling rack, slice and serve. Enjoy!

Nutrition: Carbohydrates 4.2 g / Fats 16.4 g / Protein 12.2 g / Calories 511

185. KETO "KNOCK OFF" RYE BREAD

Preparation Time: 15 minutes - Cooking Time: 1 hour - Servings: 16 slices

Ingredients : 300 g flaxseed, ground - 120 g coconut flour - 2 tbsps. caraway seeds 1 tbsp. + 1 tsp. baking powder - 5 drops liquid stevia - 32 g chia seeds 1 tsp. pink Himalayan salt - 8 eggs, separated - 110 g extra virgin olive oil 2 tbsps. toasted sesame oil - 80 ml apple cider vinegar - 240 ml warm water

Directions : Move your oven rack in the center position of your oven, then turn it on and preheat to 350 degrees Fahrenheit. Combine the first seven ingredients on your ingredients list. Mix thoroughly until the ingredients are well distributed. Set aside. To make your bread fluffier, separate the egg yolks from the whites. Set aside the whites. Combine the butter and toasted sesame oil with the yolks. Whisk the yolk mixture until it is creamy. In another bowl, whisk the egg whites until they form stiff peaks. Combine the dry ingredients with your egg yolk mixture and thoroughly mix. It will turn into coarse clumps. Add the apple cider and mix well, then add the water until thoroughly combined. Fold in the egg whites onto your batter and mix until the white disappears. Transfer your batter on a non-stick or greased lined loaf pan. Smooth the batter evenly on the pan and make a cut or indention over the batter using your spatula or wooden spoon. Place in the oven and bake for 50 to 60 minutes or until golden brown. Remove from the pan and place on a rack to cool completely. Slice and prepare a pastrami or Reuben sandwich.

Nutrition: Calories: 256 / Calories from fat: 189 / Total Fat: 21 g / Total Carbohydrates: 9 g Net Carbohydrates: 2 g / Protein: 8 g

186. KETO SOURDOUGH BAGUETTE

**Preparation Time: 10/15 minutes - Cooking Time: 50/60 minutes
Servings: 8 baguettes (about 6-inch size)**

Ingredients : 150 g almond flour - 40 g psyllium husk powder - 60 g coconut flour
75 g flax meal - 1 tsp. baking soda - 1 tsp. Himalayan pink salt - 6 large egg whites
2 large eggs - 180 g low-fat buttermilk - 60 ml apple cider vinegar - 240 ml lukewarm water

Directions : Preheat the oven to 360 degrees Fahrenheit. Scale all dry ingredients and combine them in a bowl. Mix until evenly distributed. In another bowl, mix the two eggs, the egg whites and buttermilk. The recipe is using less egg yolk so it will rise. You can save the egg yolks for other recipes. Add the egg mixture to your dry ingredients and mix using a stand mixer until it turns into a thick dough. Add the vinegar and the water and continue to mix until well combined. It should turn into a softer dough. On a baking sheet lined with parchment paper, arrange eight 6-inch elongated dough. Put space between each dough to give it room to rise. Place the baking sheet in the oven and bake for 10 minutes, then reduce the temperature to 300 degrees F before continuing to bake for another 30 to 45 minutes. Remove from the oven and place on a cooling rack to cool down completely. If it's a little moist, slice in half and toast before serving. Serve filled with roast beef and cheese or your favorite filling.

Nutrition: Calories: 232 / Calories from fat: 148 / Total Fat: 16 g / Total Carbohydrates: 14 g
Net Carbohydrates: 5 g / Protein: 12 g

187. KETO GARLIC BREAD

Preparation Time: 20 minutes - Cooking Time: 55 minutes - Servings: 16 servings

Ingredients : 1 recipe of Keto Sourdough Baguette - Garlic and Herb Butter - ½ cup softened, unsalted butter - ½ tsp pink Himalayan salt - ¼ tsp. ground black pepper - 2 tbsps. extra virgin olive oil - 4 cloves crushed garlic - 2 tbsps. fresh parsley, chopped
Toppings : ½ cup grated parmesan cheese - 2 tbsps. chopped fresh parsley

Directions : Slice the Keto sourdough baguettes in half to make 16 halves. Prepare the herb and garlic butter by mixing all ingredients until it becomes a smooth soft paste. All ingredients should reach room temperature before use. Spread about 1 to 2 teaspoons of the butter mixture on each slice of sourdough baguette. Sprinkle with parmesan cheese and parsley. Place back in the oven to crisp. Serve warm with your favorite keto pasta recipe.

Nutrition: Calories: 194 / Calories from fat: 148 / Total Fat: 16 g / Total Carbohydrates: 7 g
Net Carbohydrates: 3 g / Protein: 7 g

188. KETO ZUCCHINI BACON AND CHEESE LOAF BREAD

Preparation Time: 15 minutes - Cooking Time: 50 minutes - Servings: 12 slices

Ingredients : 3 oz. almond flour - 2 oz. coconut flour - ½ tsp. salt - ½ tsp. pepper
2 tsps. baking powder - 1 tsp. xanthan gum - 5 large eggs - 2/3 cup melted butter
4 oz. grated cheddar cheese - 6 oz. grated zucchini with water squeezed out - 6 oz. diced bacon

Directions : Preheat your oven at 350F. Using a large bowl, combine flour, salt, pepper, baking powder and xanthan gum until well mixed. Add eggs and melted butter then mix well. Fold in ¾ oz. of the cheddar, the zucchini and bacon. Mix until smooth. Transfer the batter on a loaf pan and bake for 10 to 15 minutes or until cheese turns brown. Use the toothpick test to check if already cooked. Let it cool for 20 minutes before slicing into 12 slices. Serve warm.

Nutrition: Calories: 281 / Calories from fat: 99 / Total Fat: 11 g / Total Carbohydrates: 5 g
Net Carbohydrates: 2 g / Protein: 9 g

189. KETO HAM AND CHEESE PANINI

Preparation Time: 110 minutes - Cooking Time: 40 minutes - Servings: 6 Panini

Ingredients : Bread: 1 cup +2 tbsps. warm water, divided - 1 tsp. sugar - 2 ¼ tsp. active dry yeast - 1 cup vital wheat gluten - 1 cup almond flour, super fine - ¼ cup flaxseed meal, ground
¾ tsp. salt - 1 ½ tsp. baking powder - 3 ½ tbsps. extra virgin olive oil
Panini Fillings : ½ tbsp. extra virgin olive oil - 8 slices mozzarella cheese - 8 slices sliced ham
8 slices Salami, Sopressata - 4 thin slices tomato (½ tomato)

Directions : Combine in a small bowl ½ cup of warm water, yeast and sugar. Cover the bowl with towel cloth and let it sit for 10 minutes or until bubbly. Take a large bowl and mix all the remaining dry ingredients. Sift and whisk together. Add the remaining water and olive oil in the mixture. Pour over the dry ingredients and mix well until it forms into a dough. Knead for 3 minutes then divide the dough into two equal parts. Form two tubes of dough and shape into a bread loaf about 2.5 x 7-inches. Place the dough on a greased baking sheet. Preheat the oven for 2 to 3 minutes until temperature reaches 100 to 110 degrees F. Put the dough inside the warm oven and let it rise for an hour. The dough should have risen to 3.5 x 8-inches in size. Raise the temperature of the oven to 350 degrees F to preheat. Brush the top of the dough with remaining ½ tbsp. olive oil. Place in the oven and bake for 15 minutes then take out into the oven and brush with olive oil again. Place it back in the oven and bake for another 10 to 15 minutes until the internal temperature is between 200 to 210 degrees F. Place the thermometer all the way into the loaf to get an accurate reading. Allow the loaf to cool for 30 minutes before cutting in half horizontally. Brush the outside portion of the loaf with olive oil. Start layering between the panini the 4 slices of cheese, then 4 slices salami, then 8 slices ham, then 4 slices of the remaining salami, 4 slices of tomatoes and on top layer is the remaining 4 slices of cheese. Cook in a Panini press or in a skillet over low heat for about 10 minutes or until cheese is melted and the meat is warm. Don't burn the bread. Cut the Panini into three portions and serve.

Nutrition: Calories: 542 / Calories from fat: 310 / Total Fat: 34 g / Total Carbohydrates: 12 g
Net Carbohydrates: 10 g / Protein: 49 g

190. KETO CALIFORNIA CLUB WRAP

Preparation Time: 5 minutes - Cooking Time: 5 minutes - Servings: 2

Ingredients : Wrap Ingredients : ½ cup egg whites - 2 tbsps. hemp hearts - 1/8 tsp. salt California Club : 1 tbsp. mayonnaise - 2 tbsps. fresh cilantro - 1 oz. Monterey Jack Cheese 3 oz. turkey sliced, smoked - 1 tbsp. chopped avocado - 2 tbsps. alfalfa sprouts - 1 wedge lime

Directions : To make the flatbread, mix all the ingredients in a blender until well mixed and turns into a batter in consistency. Prepare a 12-inch non-stick pan, and spray with avocado oil spray. Heat the pan over medium heat until it turns hot but not smoking. Pour the batter onto the pan then swirl the pan until it fully coated with a thin layer of the batter. Cook until golden and the top turns shiny. Flip and cook the other side for a few seconds. Transfer to a plate and start filling. Spread the mayonnaise on the wrap. Layer the filling in this order: cilantro, cheese, turkey, avocado, alfalfa. Squeeze lime over the top, and then roll lightly. Cut in half then serve.

Nutrition: Calories: 211 / Calories from fat: 120 / Total Fat: 13 g / Total Carbohydrates: 7 g Net Carbohydrates: 6 g / Protein: 17 g

191. KETO HAM AND CHEESE STROMBOLI

Preparation Time: 10 minutes - Cooking Time: 15/20 minutes - Servings: 4

Ingredients : 1 ¼ cups mozzarella shredded cheese - 4 tbsps. almond flour - 3 tbsps. coconut flour - 1 large egg - 1 tsp. Italian seasoning - 4 ounces ham, sliced - 1 ounce's cheddar cheese, sliced - Salt and pepper to taste

Directions : Preheat the oven at 400 degrees F. Combine the flours, seasoning, salt and pepper in a mixing bowl until blended. Set aside. Melt mozzarella cheese with a 10-second interval for 1 minute in the microwave, stirring occasionally. Pour melted mozzarella on your flour mixture. Allow the cheese to cool down for a minute. Add the egg but make sure the cheese has cooled down otherwise, the egg will be cooked. Mix well using a wooden spoon or spatula until it forms into a soft dough. Transfer the dough and flatten it between two sheets of parchment paper. Once flattened, use a pizza cutter to slice the dough 4-inches long from the edge to the middle. Layer the ham and cheese alternately in the middle of the dough then lift each cut part of the dough to lay it on top until you cover the ham and cheese filling. Place in the oven and bake for 15 to 20 minutes or until it turns golden brown. Cool down for about 10 minutes then slice into 4 servings.

Nutrition: Calories: 323 / Calories from fat: 200 / Total Fat: 22 g / Total Carbohydrates: 8 g Net Carbohydrates: 3 g / Protein: 23 g

192. EASY CUCUMBER BREAD

Preparation time: 10 minutes - Cooking time: 50 minutes - Servings: 6

Ingredients: 1 cup erythritol - 1 cup coconut oil, melted - 1 cup almonds, chopped - 1 teaspoon vanilla extract - A pinch of salt - A pinch of nutmeg, ground - ½ teaspoon baking powder A pinch of cloves - 3 eggs - 1 teaspoon baking soda - 1 tablespoon cinnamon powder 2 cups cucumber, peeled, deseeded and shredded - 3 cups coconut flour - Cooking spray

Directions: In a bowl, mix the flour with cucumber, cinnamon, baking soda, cloves, baking powder, nutmeg, salt, vanilla extract and the almonds and stir well. Add the rest of the ingredients except the coconut flour, stir well and transfer the dough to a loaf pan greased with cooking spray. Bake at 325 degrees F for 50 minutes, cool the bread down, slice and serve.

Nutrition: Calories 243 / Fat 12 g / Fiber 3 g / Carbs 6 g / Protein 7 g

193. GREAT BLACKBERRIES BREAD

Preparation time: 10 minutes - Cooking time: 1 hour - Servings: 10

Ingredients: 2 cups almond flour - ½ cup stevia - 1 and ½ teaspoons baking powder 1 teaspoon baking soda - 2 eggs, whisked - 1 and ½ cups almond flour - ¼ cup ghee, melted 1 tablespoon vanilla extract - 1 cup blackberries, mashed - Cooking spray

Directions: In a bowl, mix the flour with the baking powder, baking soda, stevia, vanilla and blackberries and stir well. Add the rest of the ingredients, stir the batter and pour it into a loaf pan greased with cooking spray. Bake at 400 degrees F for 1 hour, cool down, slice and serve.

Nutrition: Calories 200 / Fat 7 g / Fiber 3 g / Carbs 5 g / Protein 7 g

194. KETO RASPBERRIES BREAD

Preparation time: 10 minutes - Cooking time: 50 minutes - Servings: 6

Ingredients: 2 cups almond flour - 1 teaspoon baking soda - ¾ cup erythritol - A pinch of salt 1 egg - ¾ cup coconut milk - ¼ cup ghee, melted - 2 cups raspberries - 2 teaspoons vanilla extract - ¼ cup coconut oil, melted

Directions: In a bowl, mix the flour with the baking soda, erythritol, salt, vanilla and the raspberries and stir. Add the rest of the ingredients gradually and mix the batter well. Pour this into a lined loaf pan and bake at 350 degrees F for 50 minutes. Cool the bread down, slice and serve.

Nutrition: Calories 200 / Fat 7 g / Fiber 3 g / Carbs 5 g / Protein 7 g

195. LOW CARB YEAST BREAD

Preparation time: 10 minutes - Cooking time: 4 hours - Servings: 16 slices

Ingredients : 1 teaspoon salt - 4 tablespoons oat flour - 1 package dry yeast rapid rise/highly active - 1 1/2 teaspoons baking powder - 1/2 teaspoon sugar - 1 1/8 cups warm water 1/4 cup coarse unprocessed wheat bran 3 tablespoons olive oil - 1/4 cup flax meal 1 cup vital wheat gluten flour - 3/4 cup soy flour

Directions: Add water, yeast and sugar to the bread machine and let rest there for 10 minutes. Add the remaining ingredients and select bread mode on the machine. After the cooking time is over, remove the bread from the machine and let rest for about 10 minutes. Enjoy!

Nutrition: 99 calories / 5 g fat / 7 g total carbs / 9 g protein

196. SEEDED BREAD

Preparation time: 10 minutes - Cooking time: 40 minutes - Servings: 16 slices

Ingredients : 2 tablespoons chia seeds - 1/4 teaspoon salt - 7 large eggs - 1/2 teaspoon xanthan gum - 2 cups almond flour - 1 teaspoon baking powder - 1/2 cup unsalted butter - 3 tablespoons sesame seeds - 2 tablespoons olive oil

Directions: Add all the ingredients to the bread machine. Close the lid and choose bread mode. Once done, take out from machine and cut into at least 16 slices. This keto seeded bread can be kept for up to 4-5 days in the fridge.

Nutrition: 101 calories / 16 g fat / 4 g total carbs / 6 g protein

197. CINNAMON SWEET BREAD

Preparation time: 10 minutes - Cooking time: 1 hour - Servings: 12

Ingredients : 3 teaspoons ground cinnamon - 1 ½ cups of almond flour - 3 large eggs ½ cup keto sweetener - 1 teaspoon vanilla essence - ¼ cup coconut flour - ¼ cup sour cream 1 teaspoon baking powder - ½ cup unsweetened almond milk - ½ cup unsalted butter, melted

Directions: Add all ingredients to the bread machine. Close the lid and choose the sweet bread mode. After the cooking time is over, remove the bread from the machine and let rest for about 10 minutes. Enjoy!

Nutrition: 191 calories / 17 g fat / 5 g total carbs / 5 g protein

198. NUT AND SEED BREAD

Preparation time: 35 minutes - Cooking time: 45 minutes - Servings: 16 slices

Ingredients : 1 cup pumpkin seeds - 1 teaspoon salt - 1/2 cup almond flour - 4 eggs, whisked 1/2 cup whole almonds - 1 tablespoon lemon juice - 1 cup raw pecans - ¼ cup olive oil - 1/2 cup hazelnuts - 1/4 cup poppy seeds - 1/2 cup flax meal - 1 cup sunflower seeds - 1/2 cup chia seeds

Directions: Add all the ingredients to the bread machine. Close the lid and choose bread mode. Once done, take out from machine and cut into at least 16 slices.

Nutrition: 316 calories / 28 g fat / 11 g total carbs / 11 g protein

199. ALMOND BREAD LOAF

Preparation time: 10 minutes - Cooking time: 3 hours 22 minutes - Servings: 15

Ingredients: 2 ½ cups almond flour 1/3 cup coconut flour - ½ teaspoon xanthan gum 1 ½ teaspoons baking powder - ¼ teaspoon salt Sesame seeds - ¼ cup butter, melted and cooled 5 eggs - 2/3 cup almond milk - ¼ teaspoon tartar cream

Directions: Add all the ingredients to the bread machine. Close the lid and choose bread mode. Once done, take out from machine and cut into at least 16 slices.

Nutrition: 215 calories / 10.1 g fat / 5 g total carbs / 25.2 g protein

200. SUGAR FREE BANANA BREAD

Preparation time: 10 minutes - Cooking time: 3 hours 18 minutes - Servings: 8

Ingredients: 1 ½ cups almond flour - ¼ cup granulated erythritol sweetener 1 teaspoon baking powder - 2 teaspoons cinnamon - ¼ cup walnuts, crushed - ½ cup banana, mashed 2 tablespoons butter, melted - 3 eggs

Directions: Add all ingredients to the bread machine. Close the lid and choose the sweet bread mode. After the cooking time is over, remove the bread from the machine and let rest for about 10 minutes. Enjoy!

Nutrition: 205 calories / 17.2 g fat / 6.4 g total carbs / 8 g protein

CONCLUSION

Keto bread is not just another keto recipe. It's a balanced low carb bread that can be used as a meal replacement.Each of the issues is a suggestion that your body is in ketosis.

These are a few of the signs you will observe as you begin the transition:

You may experience keto flu or induction flu, which includes let down mental functions and energy. You may suffer from sleeping problems, bouts of nausea, augmented hunger, or other possible gastrointestinal worries. Several days into the keto plan should remedy these effects. If not, add ½ of a teaspoon of salt into a glass of water and drink it to help with the side effects. For the first week, you may need to do this daily. It could take up to 15 to 20 minutes before it helps. It will improve with time.

You may also notice an aroma similar to nail polish. Not surprising because this is acetone, a ketone product. It may also give you a unique body odor as your body adjusts to the diet changes. Maintain good oral health and use a breath refresher if needed.

Leg cramps may be an issue as you begin ketosis. The loss of magnesium (a mineral) can be a demon and create a bit of pain with the onset of the keto diet plan changes. With the loss of the minerals during urination, you could experience bouts of cramps in your legs.

Of course, the keto diet also has benefits that include:

Remain Satiated: Fat and protein are more filling and will stick to your ribs longer than products that are occupied with carbohydrates.

Dravet Syndrome: Dravet Syndrome is a severe form of epilepsy marked by prolonged, uncontrollable, and frequent seizures, which began in infancy. Unfortunately, available medications don't improve symptoms in approximately one-third of the Dravet Syndrome patients.

A clinical study used 13 children with Dravet Syndrome to stay on the ketogenic diet for more than one year to remain seizure-free. Over 50% of the group decreased in the frequency of the seizures. Six of the patients stopped the diet later, and one remains seizure-free.

Mental Focus: Your brain is approximately 60% fat by weight. By increasing your fatty food intake, you will have a better focus. It can maintain itself and work at total capacity.

Blood Pressure Levels Lowered: When you begin the ketogenic diet, your blood pressure may become lower, making you feel dizzy at first. Don't worry or feel overly concerned because that's a clear indication that the carbohydrates are working. However, if you are currently taking medications, it's a good idea to speak with your physician about the possibility of lowering some of your doses while on the ketogenic or intermittent fasting plan.

Polycystic Ovary Syndrome (PCOS): Young women of childbearing years can be affected by this disorder. It is further also associated with obesity, insulin resistance, and hyperinsulinemia. One study concluded a significant improvement in weight loss in fasting women over 24-weeks. The group limited carb intake to 20 grams daily for 24 weeks, which led to its success.

There are many more benefits, but you now have a good idea of how much better you can feel if you follow the keto techniques of dieting.